# STOP GIVING
# *Start Living!*

## From Burnout to Chillout

A journey from stress and exhaustion,
to finding calm in today's busy world

## Emma J Mathews

# Testimonials

"Emma's lived experiences impart wisdom to all people who are hustling in today's fast paced and high demand society. This is a must-read book for those who are suffering from burnout. I would definitely recommend this to my clients."

**Dr Gloria Lee,
Psychologist, Professor of Counselling Psychology,
University of British Columbia**

"We need more women speaking up about the realities of modern motherhood and womanhood. Too many of us are silent, thinking we're the only ones struggling. Emma is not one of those women. She is brave enough to take her lived experience of burn out and motherhood and share it with the world - not only in the hope of shining a light on the issue, but to also provide real and tested steps back out of it. This book is important and much needed for so many."

**Amy Taylor-Kabbaz,
Author and Coach, Happy Mama Movement
Sydney, Australia**

"Emma shows us the healing value of rest and self-connection in a world that rewards the opposite. To pause means to be open and vulnerable enough to feel. Like Emma, we have to courageously feel and move through our suffering to find our own embodied truth. After reading Emma's authentic personal story, I am left imagining an awakened world where the yoga of self-awareness restores the balance and heals an unconscious collective trauma."

**Kendra Boone,
Trauma-Sensitive Yoga and Embodiment Facilitator,
Canberra, Australia**


"Emma's raw account of her burnout and path to repair delivers a lesson on the value of tranquillity. Drawing on age-old practices including yoga, breath work and repair through relaxation, Emma found a counterpoint to modern day expectations which brought her body and mind back to functional peace. If you have lost your way, this book and Emma's path may just help you find it."

**Ruth G Wright,
PhD (Psych); Dru Yoga Teacher,
Canberra, Australia**


"I think it is so incredibly brave of Emma to share her story. So many people feel alone in not being able to 'keep up' with the fast pace that society seems to insist on. It's a trap that many fall into, especially those who have University qualifications and professional careers like Emma. When a person shares their story with the Community it gives others a chance to see that they are not alone, it reminds me of

Brene Brown's powerful words, 'One day you will tell your story of how you overcame what you went through and it will be someone else's survival guide.' This is Emma turning around and offering a hand to all women and mothers who have reached burnout. This is Emma offering her heart and sharing her very own survival guide. If you need permission, I give it to you. 'Take her hand'. What a gift."

**Kelly Wolf,**
**Sacred Union Embodiment Founder,**
**Batemans Bay, NSW**

First published by Ultimate World Publishing 2021
Copyright © 2021 Emma Mathews

ISBN

Paperback: 978-1-922597-81-6
Ebook: 978-1-922597-82-3

Emma Mathews has asserted her rights under the Copyright, Designs and Patents Act 1988 to be identified as the author of this work. The information in this book is based on the author's experiences and opinions. The publisher specifically disclaims responsibility for any adverse consequences which may result from use of the information contained herein. Permission to use information has been sought by the author. Any breaches will be rectified in further editions of the book.

All rights reserved. No part of this publication may be reproduced, stored in or introduced into a retrieval system, or transmitted in any form, or by any means (electronic, mechanical, photocopying, recording or otherwise) without the prior written permission of the author. Any person who does any unauthorised act in relation to this publication may be liable to criminal prosecution and civil claims for damages. Enquiries should be made through the publisher.

**Cover design:** Ultimate World Publishing
**Layout and typesetting:** Ultimate World Publishing
**Editor:** Alex Floyd-Douglass
**Cover Photo:** Taken from Adventure Bay on Bruny Island, looking north towards the Tasman Peninsula, Tasmania.

Ultimate World Publishing
Diamond Creek,
Victoria Australia 3089
www.writeabook.com.au

# Dedication

To all the givers – you know who you are.

# Contents

| | |
|---|---|
| Preface | xi |
| Note from the Author | xiii |
| Introduction | 1 |
| Chapter One: Crash and Burn | 13 |
| Chapter Two: A Shattered Life | 21 |
| Chapter Three: Trapped in the Darkness | 33 |
| Chapter Four: The Stress of STEMM | 43 |
| Chapter Five: Burnout Mama Life | 55 |
| Chapter Six: The 2020 Cauldron | 71 |
| Chapter Seven: Unlocking Life's Lessons | 83 |
| Chapter Eight: Healing Together | 95 |
| Chapter Nine: My Recovery Secrets | 111 |
| Chapter Ten: Living Not Giving | 127 |
| Chapter Eleven: Chillout Inspiration | 139 |
| Chapter Twelve: From Burnt Out to Chilled Out | 157 |
| Afterword | 167 |
| References | 169 |
| Appendix A: Resources | 173 |
| About the Author | 175 |
| Acknowledgements | 177 |
| Offers for burnout recovery | 179 |
| Speaker Bio | 183 |
| Freelance Work | 185 |
| Final Word | 189 |

# Preface

*"Loving ourselves through the process of owning our story is the bravest thing we will ever do."*

(Brene Brown)

# Note from the Author

*I have deliberately obscured some identifying features of characters in this book for both legal and moral reasons. In some instances, dates, locations and other identifiers have been changed to protect those that need protecting. All names have been changed. The events recounted in this text are based on my thoughts and feelings as I felt them at the time. Descriptions are backed by actual life events. No ill-will or offence is intended to any of the participants involved.*

*In telling my story, I am cognisant that I write my story only. I do not presume to tell the story of others who feature in this book. Their feelings, emotions, thoughts and memories are their own and they deserve the respect I give them, by only writing about them what is necessary in telling my own story. This is my perspective only.*

*This book may trigger painful memories and or strong reactions, please seek help if this occurs. You can find contact details and assistance if you require it in **Appendix A** at the back of this book.*

# Introduction

*"Going inward. That's the real work. The solutions are not outside of us. Get to know who you really are, because as you search for the hero within, you inevitably become one."*

(Emma Tiebens)

Do you feel like you are running on empty? Drained and energy-less? Or like you are on a treadmill of juggling everything and constantly giving?

You might be overwhelmed and overworked and feel simply exhausted from the demands of daily life.

When managing home and work life seems like a 24/7 marathon – or when our to-do list is never really done – we start to feel the heaviness of all those commitments bearing down on us. Sometimes it seems like there's no end in sight, but more work and more stress.

When the life that we lead starts to become too much, stress and overwhelm set in. Then burnout and fatigue are next if that stress doesn't get managed.

And that's what happened to me.

When I was younger, I can remember friends and family used to say I was 'down to earth'. To me, this meant I was grounded and had an inner calm deep within myself. But somewhere during my education, I changed and lost that grounding.

During university, I became more easily stressed and anxious. The pressure of success and achievement weighed heavily on me. I wanted to do well and enjoyed the feeling of success and the accolades. My ego relished the attention of distinctions and high marks.

But there was a cost to my inner calm and I lost sight of what my true needs were.

That was the point that I started to 'buy in' to all the societal expectations. The goal-setting, achievement-getting pace of the masculine world I had been initiated into. I was unaware of just how draining on my energy that would be. Until burnout.

I used to be so energetic and outgoing that I was rarely still.

I was always on the look-out for new opportunities and adventures. I went bushwalking and visited exciting places, like Iceland, Vanuatu, Turkey and Indonesia. I enjoyed

## Introduction

getting out of my comfort zone and meeting people. But after immersing myself in a demanding job for a few years, I lost sight of all that and forgot to look after myself and my inner needs.

I was working long hours and wasn't giving myself enough time to relax and de-stress.

Although I had an intense workload, I thought I was adequately dealing with the pressure of it all. But in reality, I was slowly but surely becoming tired and worn out. I didn't notice that stress was building up, because I was operating on autopilot. I tried to get through each day and typical tasks I'd usually do with ease, but I was getting more and more run-down. I didn't recognise that the life I was living, was wearing me out – until it was too late.

I had become so accustomed to pushing myself, that I was just surviving.

At the time, I was working in a demanding professional role. I supervised surveillance equipment and computer systems, often alone. I had multiple responsibilities to manage, which over time, became too much for me to handle on my own.

I had begun to feel more and more mentally and physically exhausted.

*In the months leading up to burnout, my energy levels were at an all-time low. I felt so depleted and drained. I found the act of doing anything and everything, was a real struggle. Managing normal daily tasks were getting more and more difficult.*

I found that I was becoming anxious and stressed before even getting to work. Then, when I got there, I felt tense and jittery and found it hard to focus on one thing. I felt disconnected from work. I felt tightness and tension in my face and across my forehead that didn't ease. When I wasn't there, work was on my mind, so the stress I was holding didn't get a chance to subside.

I couldn't wind down and relax enough on my time off. I wasn't giving myself what I needed.

These were all warning signs, but I didn't recognise them as such, until it was too late. I could no longer manage anymore. I didn't have anything else to give. Eventually, just getting through the day without crumbling became a regular achievement.

We now know that workplace burnout is caused by prolonged or excessive stress that results in mental, physical and emotional exhaustion. (Smith et al., 2020)

# Introduction

That was exactly what I was going through. The World Health Organisation recently relabelled burnout as an "occupational phenomenon." (WHO, 2019)

The primary causes of burnout are understood to be long-lasting and poorly managed workplace stress, along with more overtime and administrative work. (Robinson, 2019)

I was unaware that this could happen at the time.

I didn't know that overwork, extreme busyness and the everyday stress I experienced, could build-up to make me sick. I didn't know our body and mind could reach its limit if we put too much pressure on it, or if we weren't gentle enough on ourselves. But that's what happened.

The life I lived had become too much.

I couldn't satisfy all the demands and expectations I had any more. I had given too much and needed to start to put myself first. For the sake of my health and wellbeing.

Prior to suffering burnout in 2016, I had gone through an extended period of stress in my job and wasn't sleeping well. Combined with some challenges in my personal life, I was overdoing it. I knew deep down that the responsibilities and demands of my work were draining me too much. I was working long hours and if needed, I also did overtime.

When I asked for help to manage the challenges I was going through, my complaints and appeals were brushed aside.

I sensed that by asking for help I was being 'too soft', too needy and vulnerable. But I badly needed help.

Ultimately, my requests for help were ignored and put in the 'too hard' basket. So, the stress and exhaustion I was contending with, wasn't resolved or managed. Also, the lack of support made me doubt my own inner knowledge. Made me feel that I wasn't tough enough or strong enough.

But the all-encompassing mental and physical exhaustion I felt was telling me otherwise.

If you are reading this book, I'm sure you are all too aware of how much is asked of us in today's workplaces. Overwork, stress and burnout is something many full-time workers have to contend with (not out of choice, I'm sure). A 2019 Gallup study found that two thirds of full-time workers experienced burnout at work. (Robinson, 2019)

Add in working from home and we are under more stress than ever before. Not surprisingly, as many as four in five Australians suffered from burnout during 2020. (Johnson, 2021)

At the time, this made Australia one of the countries with the highest rate of burnout globally.

The continual intense stress I felt, meant that my adrenal glands weren't functioning very well, giving me adrenal fatigue.

If we are under continual stress, over time our adrenal glands burn out from long-term cortisol production. (Whitbourne, 2021)

## Introduction

Adrenaline and cortisol are released as a reaction to stress. When this happens, these hormones give us a 'fight or flight', emergency response, when we sense danger. If felt continuously this can result in anxiety – which is something else burnout gave me!

*Burnout is hard to explain to others who haven't experienced it, because I did not have any outward physical signs of being unwell. I had reduced overall energy levels and had this constant feeling of fatigue that just didn't get better with more sleep.*

Burnout affected my sense of self, my personal wellbeing, my energy and resilience. I felt disinterested in social engagement and it reduced my productivity at work. It also led to issues with my sleep and mood and mental health issues, such as anxiety.

Even though burnout happened to me five years ago, I still experience burnout symptoms.

To this day, I find it hard to relax and de-stress, and I can also feel jittery and on edge in busy or social situations. I find it especially difficult when there's a series of closely spaced, or stressful tasks that I need to manage – particularly when I don't get enough time to have a break in between each one.

Burnout has been a journey of personal growth for me.

Although I didn't seek it out and couldn't accept it; it was and still is, life-changing. Once I had accepted the hand I was dealt and the personal change that I was going through, I could begin a personal transformation. I could look deeper and go inward to find out what my real needs are and not what had been told, or expected of me.

Burnout woke me up to the energy-draining effects of the modern world.

The world can be a demanding and harmful place, if we don't look after ourselves and protect our personal wellbeing. The only way we can protect ourselves is to give ourselves kindness and self-compassion amid all the hype and busyness.

I truly lacked a gentleness and kindness with myself before burnout. I expected a lot and gave a lot. But since burnout, my attitude towards my own self-care has deepened. I value it so much more.

It seems that we are always so busy in today's world, stillness is a bit of a rarity.

The modern world can be such a busy place with so many things pulling at us. We're expected to constantly compete and achieve and operate at a hectic pace. Our never-ending to-do-lists, plans and endless tasks at home and work keep us continually busy. As our perpetual commitments of satisfying the expectations of others and our own ambitions

## Introduction

dominate our days, we rarely give ourselves time to stop and do nothing.

It is becoming harder and harder to switch off, as 24/7 access to smartphones and emails often invade our relaxation and chillout time.

*We rarely take enough meaningful breaks to calm our nervous systems. We hardly ever allow ourselves the act of non-doing – to breathe deeply, relax and be still. So, let's not forget to gaze at that beautiful flower in the garden, or simply watch the clouds passing by overhead. To calm our nervous energy and to make more time for stillness before burnout creeps up.*

It's so important that we find space for stillness and boredom in this crazy world.

Now, I can see that I didn't give myself enough time for stillness before burnout because I was operating on autopilot. I didn't allow myself time to 'smell the roses', so to speak, to take the time to just breathe and be content with non-doing. I wasn't mindful of the implications of how I lived and how that lifestyle could potentially impact on my health and wellbeing. I had my eyes closed and lacked true self-awareness.

Living my life on autopilot was like being asleep at the wheel of life.

As professionals and mamas in today's world, I believe we are finding it increasingly hard to say no to those extra tasks that are put on us. There seems to be an endless stream of responsibilities, commitments and expectations to satisfy, from both our families and workplace. It never ends – believe me, I know.

To say no to some of these things can be really hard to do. Especially when we can see a beneficial outcome for others, for our children, for our employer, or ourselves and our own ambitions. It takes inner strength, courage and self-belief to take that kind of action. But we can often feel pushed to our limits, like we have nothing else to give. It's those times, when we are running on empty, that we really, really need to say no. For the good of our health and wellbeing. Saying 'no' is a proactive step along the path to self-care and developing some new positive habits despite all the 'busy', because it won't simply go away. Put yourself first, and believe that in saying 'no', you are being kind to yourself.

We are constantly giving.

Absorbed in busyness, we forget to connect with ourselves, to check in on our own needs. Then add being a mama into the mix and it's a recipe for even more stress and overwhelm. We are all so busy as mamas, but for a person with burnout, it gets compounded. That was (and often still is) the position I was faced with – a mama with low energy and easily stressed, with a new child. Add in juggling part

# Introduction

time work, where we end up giving more time to work than is allocated. With so many others' needs to satisfy; we often forget that we also need a bit of time for self-care.

We need to check in and give more to ourselves, to replenish and recharge, otherwise the cycle of always doing, busyness and high stress will continue.

Becoming a mama as well as suffering burnout, has only made me become stronger in my self-awareness and outlook on giving more to myself, in order to live the life I want.

*Overworking, being busy and always doing, are often worn like a badge of honour in today's world.*

But that comes at a cost to our health and wellbeing. I believe burnout is a hidden epidemic in our modern society. It's not discussed openly and brushed aside because we feel a sense of failure or shame about what we couldn't achieve or succeed at. A sense that we can't meet our commitments and the demands that the modern world has asked of us. But it is a real problem that many of us have to deal with: from professionals to mamas and those who juggle multiple commitments.

If we don't talk about it, if we don't openly accept it is an all too common, unfair reality, then it will keep happening.

It's important to share our common stories and learn from each other. We don't need to be perfect. We just need to be not stressed and not burnt out.

This is why I'm sharing my story.

For years after burnout, I retreated from the world. I felt like I failed in my career and my life and felt ashamed that burnout happened to me. So, I kept it hidden in the dark. I felt as if this wasn't meant to be the way my life went. But it did and I fully accept that. Now, I feel comfortable to reveal the true story of my dark side. It's a vulnerable story of the real things that I experienced in my journey through burnout.

It's a journey of learning, personal growth and transformation. I'd like to empower sufferers of burnout more with my real-world solutions and chillout hacks – to give them what I've learnt through my recovery. My insights and practical solutions are a helping hand and offer of practical guidance, so they don't have to go it alone to overcome burnout.

I have always been a giver. Now, I want to give my story to help and support those who think they are on the road to burnout – or are already there.

## Chapter One

# Crash and Burn

*"It's nice to look back on your life and see things as lessons and not regrets."*

(Rihanna)

I was a woman in her 30s with a demanding professional career in Science Technology Engineering Mathematics and Medicine (STEMM). I had a role that required long work hours, mainly alone. I was working a roster with 12-hour day and night shifts doing surveillance, which involved 24/7 monitoring of sensors, equipment and computer systems. The shifts were pretty full on and demanding physically on my health – and mentally on my analytical skills. I was pushing myself hard and was under a lot of stress in that role.

Combined with that, I also had some stress in my personal life. I split up with a long-term partner – which was a positive change for me – but I think it left me struggling a little bit finding my way in the world alone. So, I filled in the emptiness and loneliness by going out a lot. I spent time with people out of the house, going out with friends and meeting new people. It was positive in that way, but looking back, I think I was feeling unbalanced and ungrounded within myself.

I tried to get support to leave that role, but I struggled to get any traction with that. After discussing my needs with several managers, it came to nothing and I had to stay put in a job that was really pushing me to my limits.

One of the things I did to fill that loneliness I felt, was get a dog. She was a great friend and buddy for me while at home in an otherwise empty house. She was a fun Kelpie-cross and very active. She needed regular exercise and to run every day, which was very full on for a single person with a demanding job. I thought I could handle a dog, being active myself. But I started to find that I couldn't keep up with her needs, along with my job. I was out of the house for long work shifts and this led to her escaping through the fence a few times. It all became too stressful. I had to solve the problem, but I couldn't fix the fence myself. I considered tying her up during the day, but that didn't sit well with me. So, she continued escaping and stressing me out, over and over again.

## Burnout Warning Signs

There were several precursors to me burning out that I can recognise now, when I look back at that time. I was crying a lot. I just had a lot of emotion to release that I now believe was stress and overwhelm. When I cried; I couldn't really stop crying. It was hard to accept feeling this way. I wasn't sleeping well because of the shift work job that I had, which left me with a sleep issue. I struggled with sleep a lot, because of the impacts on my sleeping patterns. So, a lot of days I would wake up in the morning feeling exhausted. I really needed sleep to help me recover from the demands of work, but I wasn't getting it.

One time I can remember, I had some tickets to a music concert. As I said, I was going out a lot at that time and it was a band that I really wanted to see. My friend had bought me a ticket and I realised the day of the concert that I just didn't want to leave the house. I was so emotional. I was sitting on the couch crying. I was upset with myself for not feeling like I could go, even though I wanted to. I was torn between spending time with my friend and looking after myself. So, I called her and was crying uncontrollably when we spoke, but she was very supportive and said, *"Look, if you don't feel like going, just don't go in Emma."* I was so grateful for her care and understanding at that time.

It was moments like these that helped me get through tough times when I was struggling. These small glimpses of care were like a warm light of comfort amongst everything else. Especially when I was wading through a mire of fatigue and emotional despair. These moments gave me the strength and courage, so I believed I could move forward, grow and get through this thing I was experiencing, called burnout.

## The Night I Crashed

My dog had escaped on a long day shift. Then after the day shift, I had two or three days off work to relax and wind down. But although I felt low on energy – I didn't know how low I truly was. There were chores to be done, shopping and housework, all the usual stuff. Then after those two or three days off, I was due to start night shifts, but I just didn't feel like I had the energy or the stamina or the strength to go into work.

In addition to the work, I was in the office on my own at night time, which is a little bit stressful for a woman. It was just me and the security guard. I was usually fine when I got there, but that night I just couldn't face it.

At that point, I needed help. I knew I couldn't go into work that night, so eventually after a lot of self-questioning, tension and stress (it was hard for me to make a good decision feeling stressed like I was), late in the afternoon I called my boss to say I didn't feel I could make it. She asked me to call another colleague to fill in for me on that shift.

So even on that phone call, I wasn't helped.

I was already doing so much on my own and as a giver, I didn't feel comfortable saying *"no"* – I wasn't used to it.

And when I called to ask for help, the onus was put back onto me to help myself again. I got the impression that she thought I was making excuses, so I could get out of work and maybe I wasn't explicit enough about how I felt at the time. But I really felt alone in my suffering; in what I was going through. That made me even more stressed out and I ended up feeling quite distressed by it all.

*Looking back, I think I was feeling a high level of anxiety. My thoughts were racing, my heart was beating really quickly and I was breathing rapidly, plus I had a tightness in my stomach and across my forehead.*

I tried to rest after not going to that night shift, so I could get ready for the next one. But, it was hard to slow down and stop my racing thoughts. I could hardly sleep I was so wound up.

I didn't have the tools I needed to calm down. I didn't know how. Plus, I was so tense and anxious after days of build-up. I still hadn't recovered enough to go to the next shift. So I called in sick for that shift as well. However, my manager said, "Look, we can't fill that shift Emma, can you come into work?"

As the giving person I was at the time, I let my manager convince me to go into work against my body and my mind screaming at me, telling me not to.

I drove into work fuming.

I can remember that night so well even now. I wasn't driving very safely on the road into work. I had my loud music pumping that I would normally use to get me motivated, but it was only making me feel more stressed. I was very angry and upset with my manager and also with myself, for even going into work.

When I got there, I felt on edge and stressed, like my brain was breaking. At some point, early in the night (the shift started about 6.30pm) I started crying. I just started crying and I couldn't stop. As I was on my own, my only option was to call someone for help, to seek their advice as I wasn't thinking clearly. I wasn't sure what to do.

So, I ended up calling a very close friend, who gave me some great advice. She told me to just call another colleague to see if they could come in to relieve me from the shift, so I could go home to rest. So that's what I did.

Thankfully the colleague I called could come in to help. I was crying when I spoke to this person. I mean, it was a professional role and I hate the thought that I was crying in front of this person, but I honestly couldn't stop myself. It was just an explosion of emotion. A release of stress and everything that I had been through.

I'm so thankful for the friend who was there to able to pick up the phone when I needed her. I'm also really grateful to my colleague who came in and helped me that night. It was an extremely hard time to get through and not something

I could have done on my own, in the catastrophic state I was in.

If I could do it all again, I would have valued myself more.

I would have understood the importance of placing myself in high esteem and believed that I was worthy. If I had valued my wellbeing then I would have stuck up for myself and said "no" to my manager that night, with the intention of a person who felt strongly about taking care of her own health. I should have spoken up at that point and not allowed her to tread all over me. To convince me that way, when deep down I knew what was best for me. I knew what I was and wasn't capable of. The trouble was, I didn't act on those feelings and stand up for myself.

No-one else knew how I felt. Only me.

At that time, I think I needed guidance but there was no-one who was there who could offer that. Being alone made me realise how little self-belief and confidence I had in myself. I was struggling with my new normal at the time and wish I could have asked for help from my close friends, a psychologist or life coach to help navigate my life then.

We can't live our lives alone and separate ourselves from the help of others.

We don't have to be strong on our own, but I acted as if I was tough and strong. I thought I was. Based on my past experience, I thought I could get through anything life dished out to me. But I hadn't come across anything like this before. I needed to be ok with being vulnerable and ask for help earlier, to get through the huge challenges I was facing. If only I knew then what I know now, I would do a lot of things differently. And maybe, just maybe, I could have avoided burnout altogether...

Someone once told me that as individuals we can handle three things. They could be anything: such as a deadline at work, relationship issues or a sick child. But if we get another challenge to deal with on top of what we are already contending with, it can become overwhelming. We all have challenges in our lives, but it's the fourth thing that can push us to our limits.

All of a sudden, we have too much on our plate.

I think something like that happened to me. I was dealing with being on my own in the world, with a demanding job that generated stress, along with sleep issues. Then on top of all that, my dog started escaping, which was the last straw that pushed me beyond my limits and into burnout.

## Chapter Two

# A Shattered Life

*"Just because you have a failure, it does not mean that you are a failure. So fail gently, gracefully, bravely."*

(Tamara Levitt)

After the crash and burn happened, I felt completely different to how I felt before. Like my life had been totally shattered and broken apart from what I'd been through. It was a strange place to be, like I was in a world of fog and numbness where I just couldn't take any new input or stimuli. It seemed like I had lost my energy supply; I was so, so tired. I was mentally hazy and just couldn't think clearly or maintain focus.

So, naturally, I retreated away from the world.

I felt on edge and even a tiny amount of stimulation would trigger feelings of anxiety and the fight or flight response. My body was tense, which I felt in my face, shoulders and stomach. Combined with all that, I wasn't sleeping well, which hindered my recovery and ability to relax properly.

## Burning Feelings

I felt certain physical sensations if I was overstimulated or too busy for prolonged periods with no break. I would just get wound up in my body. I would feel tension in my face, around my mouth and around my eyes. For example, I would get a twitchy upper lip. Sometimes one of my eyelids or eyebrows would twitch on its own.

It took me a while to notice the link between those physical sensations and being too busy or overstimulated. But once I had tuned in and started to notice, I could say there was a link between being too busy, being too active, having too many tasks on and a physical sensation that would actually be telling me that I needed to stop or to have a rest.

When I first returned to work right after it had happened, if I had been focusing on something very intensely for a long period of time, I would feel these sensations. I would also start to feel tension when I was talking to people, especially in a big group. I started to notice that I would just begin to lose interest in a conversation and become unfocused. That was the sign that I needed to take a break.

## A Shattered Life

*I think I had been ignoring signs of stress and overwork for a few months leading up to my burnout because of the way it crept up on me.*

It's taken me a long time to get to this point, I find that I'm still tuning in and learning about myself and my needs as time goes on, now five years after burnout.

Straight after my burnout, I had to keep a very tight control on myself and the things I did to avoid feeling those sensations. I didn't like to feel them because they reminded me of that night and what I went through on my own. I had specific needs that really had to be met or I would go backwards into a world of stress, tension and anxiety.

I just couldn't be busy. I couldn't be in loud noise.

It was as though things had to be in just the right balance for me to function or I would start to feel the tension and stress in my body and face. I felt I had to have a 'sweet spot' where everything in my surroundings had to be just right and comfortable, at that point in time. I think I needed that at the time, so I could recover bit by bit.

My recovery was gradual and slow. I spent weeks feeling like I didn't make any improvement at all.

After I began to improve, I started to feel like I wasn't pushing myself as much. It was a massive step and I started to feel more positive and reassured. It started to be ok for me to get out of my comfort zone bit by bit.

I used to tell myself, *"It's okay to be in busy situations sometimes, it's okay to be in loud noise sometimes."*

It was a whole process overcoming that fear of putting myself in certain situations again without feeling like I was risking my health and taking big steps backwards into those horrible persistent sensations of burnout that I felt after it first happened. But I did it and got out of the hole I was in. I achieved it, learned to overcome my fears and get okay with feeling discomfort again. I'm okay with discomfort now if it's not impacting me negatively. I got there thankfully.

But I still feel I'm still on that journey a bit, even today.

I need to remind myself of my limitations. Remind myself that it may seem as if I'm handling a stressful or busy situation, but I might not be. I now check in with myself regularly to see if I can notice any signs of feeling stressed. Because it catches up with me later in how long it takes me to wind down and de-stress. There are repercussions for my family and relationships if I don't notice the signs.

In the worst-case scenario, it can take days to de-stress and shake off the tension through consistent sleep, meditation, having a calm approach and limiting my activities. If I notice a build-up of stress happening and can escape from the stressor, then it's much less. That's what I try to aim for these days. It's better for everyone that way.

**Interrupted Sleep**

Before I burnt out, I was doing long hours at work and shift work. I already had disruptions to my sleeping patterns beforehand, but after burnout, I was trying to recover from existing sleep issues that were leftover from that job. This was challenging because I really, really needed sleep to recover. I needed rest to get over it, but shift work had disrupted my sleep patterns and circadian rhythms so much.

It's taken years to get on top of my sleep problems. I'd had some issues with restful sleep because of my family history anyway. My mum has had her share of sleep disruptions and often used to lay awake at night unable to rest due to an overactive mind. Then in mid-life hormonal ups and downs affected her sleep for several years. Her mum – my grandma – has also had disrupted sleep for many years. She thinks it first began after she had children and never regained a good pattern after they grew up. Then, after suddenly losing a close family member, she believes the stress of that added to it. Now in her 80s, she still survives on just four or five hours sleep a night, due to pain and discomfort.

So, there are some unstable sleep patterns in my family. I know everyone copes with disruption to their sleep differently, but I think that I was very sensitive to sleep disruptions in that job, which is why it took me such a long time to improve my overall sleeping at night time after I left.

Sometimes I couldn't relax enough to go to sleep. That was at its worst, usually after a really busy day where I'd had a lot of different tasks on. It was a little while after the burnout occurred that I realised – or someone told me – that if you don't have little points of relaxation throughout the day, it affects how well or how capable you are of relaxing at the end of the day.

For example, if I had a class or something on after work, it was too much for me after burnout. So, I gave up extracurricular activities and commitments after work, so I could go home and have adequate time to unwind before going to bed.

Often with my sleep problems, I would just be there sitting up in bed at night with insomnia, not being able to get to sleep. I used to sit in bed and put some relaxing music on my phone. I would only look at my phone for a fleeting moment - so as not to let the blue light stimulate me - and just close my eyes and listen to relaxing music. I also started to do some meditation through an app, which helped me relax more before sleep.

Sometimes, something strange would happen where I would be tired at around 9pm, but when I went to bed, my body would wake up. I think my whole circadian clock was out of whack after that job when I had to be awake and alert at night. So, it took a long time to get my night time sleep patterns and routine back to normal.

One thing I discovered that used to help, was to look at the blue sky during the day without sunglasses on. When you look at the blue sky during the day, your body clock knows its daytime, and therefore when it comes to night time, your body knows it needs to get ready for sleep. It seems simple when we do it as a natural part of our day. But shift work made me better understand what my body needed in order to sleep well again.

*Sometimes my mind would become very active and I found that if I'd had a really busy day, it was really hard to switch my brain off. Meditation was really the one way that I could calm my active mind, so I could slow down enough to sleep.*

To this day, after a busy day I will do a longer meditation that usual to help me wind down. My standard meditations are 10-15 minutes long, however, on busy days I try to do up to half an hour.

I know there's no point putting my head on the pillow for sleep when I'm feeling agitated, because I just won't sleep. If I'm not relaxed enough and when my mind is racing, meditation really helps to reset and calm my active brain and settle the jittery sensations in my body. I found this such a valuable tool to restore a sense of calm and recentre myself.

## Anxiously Out and About

After burnout, I held a lot of fears and one of the biggest ones was of the workplace where it had occurred. The first time I went in to work after it happened, I felt very tense and anxious. Being there stressed me out so much that I started crying. I was there for probably an hour and just had to fill in some forms and do some minor administrative tasks. But once I got there, I realised that I couldn't stay at my desk or even be in the building. It was stressful and just too much for me to deal with. I couldn't focus on my tasks and felt self-conscious crying in the office. It wasn't right. Feeling like that really took me by surprise.

I felt scared to be at work. I guess I was feeling the fight or flight response in my body. My mind was saying, *"Get out of here, this a dangerous place for you."*

I also had a fear of big shopping centres, busy situations with crowds, such as airports – anywhere with lots of things going on. Shops with loud music and a lot of background noise were really stressful on me. I realised these places were overstimulating environments – there's a lot of sensory input in shopping centres, to get customers to buy things. They have this loud intrusive music going to make people think faster, which is the exact effect it had on me. I think my mind was going at full speed and on overdrive so I couldn't focus or think clearly, which then made me feel more stressed and anxious.

That is the intention of the music – to speed you up to the point where you're not thinking straight when you make a purchase. But for someone with a stress response and getting through burnout, it had a negative effect.

I used to enjoy shopping. But ever since, I only go to the shops in small doses now.

I used to feel comfortable in shopping centres, but since my burnout, I started to do more online shopping (we are so lucky to be able to do that, aren't we?). I also started wearing earplugs at the shopping centres, cafes and in other busy environments. It just muffled the noise a little bit for me. I could still hear what was going on, but it just made it less intrusive. I didn't get that really strong stimulating input into my head and brain. So, if I wasn't thinking about how noisy it was, I was more relaxed and less anxious to look around and shop.

After burnout, I had more severe social anxiety about being in social situations. Having a more introverted personality meant that I was already the kind of person to be a bit more sensitive to that. But social situations where I was talking and concentrating on a conversation in a cafe or in a meeting (e.g. not in a safe space), became very stressful for me. I found it particularly stressful being in a group of three or more people and I would start to feel twitches on my face, tension around my eyes and feel a bit hot. I'd also start to lose focus on what people were talking about.

When I met friends out, I would try to decide on the place to meet and find venues that I knew would be quieter or where I could sit outside. It was more relaxing for me to sit outside, as I wasn't exposed to the loud music inside the venue. Even in winter, I was happy to rug up and sit outside – although I'm not sure my friends were very happy! I would also try to meet people one-on-one. I still wanted to catch up with friends, but it was hard to make them understand that I was not able to accommodate all their needs anymore.

I was a different person.

*I couldn't be the same person I used to be if I was to heal. That person wasn't tuned into my needs and didn't have self-awareness.*

I knew my brain needed time to heal and restore itself. So that's what I gave it. I was gentler with myself going forward, giving myself more time to rest, which was a big win for my recovery.

Driving was something that drained me a lot because it requires a lot of concentration. Looking behind you, checking mirrors, staying alert and on the ball – it all really stressed me out. So, I reduced the amount of driving I did.

## A Shattered Life

After I drove, I would do some focused breathing in the car before I got out to de-stress and if it was a long drive, I needed to rest afterwards.

The longest journey I did regularly was a half hour drive into work. I often used to start work already feeling worn out and stressed after the drive. But I did things like take a break once I pulled up – I didn't rush out of the car and into work anymore. I couldn't do that after burnout. But driving was something I continued to do even though it was stressful on me, so I could maintain some normality. But I avoided going places or driving unnecessarily and let my partner drive me where possible.

*I often felt frustrated because I couldn't do the things that I used to do. I had been the type of person who was always on the go. It frustrated me that I couldn't be as active and energetic.*

I was always planning things, getting out and about, and catching up with friends. I was always doing. Because of those personality traits, it wasn't an easy road to come to terms with the new sensations I felt, the sleep problems, feeling anxious out and about in the world, and in busy situations. But I got there.

Burnout slowed me down.

Thankfully, I got to the point where now I can go into a shopping centre without my earplugs. I can be in crowds and busy situations, but I always limit my time. If there's loud music on at a cafe, I'll try to sit outside or suggest an alternative location.

I think I have more courage now to ask for what I need and stand up for myself.

Learning about what I needed and speaking up for myself was a big part of the process for me to get through burnout. It was something that never used to be easy or come naturally for me. But now I know that if I don't stand up for my needs, it will come back and bite me later. The stress will affect my health and I don't want that to occur too often. My needs are just as important as anybody else's, but no-one will stand up or ask for me – I have to do that.

So, I continuously have to retrain myself and over-ride old entrenched habits to get what I want. It's an ongoing process of re-learning, but I have proved to myself that I am capable of making positive progress with that.

After all, re-learning is part of the process of moving forward.

## Chapter Three

# Trapped in the Darkness

> *"Stillness is where creativity and solutions to problems are found."*
> (Eckhart Tolle)

In addition to dealing with the immediate mental health issues and physical impacts of burnout, I had to contend with what other people thought about my condition. How others perceived my response to my health issue and the negative fallout. In addition to what I had been through, the loss of certain friends and ostracism by senior staff who didn't want to be reminded of my ordeal, was totally unexpected.

Feeling isolated and helpless without their support, left me feeling trapped, alone and carrying a huge sense of shame. A sense of shame about my problem and a sense of shame about how others saw me - as a failure.

All these external opinions highlighted what I was feeling on the inside – and amplified it. I felt trapped, in a very dark place.

## Vulnerability Misunderstood

It was a real struggle dealing with people who didn't understand what I was going through, when I felt so vulnerable. For probably the first time in my life, I knew what it felt like to be an outcast, an oddity. Judged and ignored by people who, it seemed, needed to have a quick opinion of me. I had to deal with people at work, including so-called friends, who thought what I had was a mindset problem.

It was as if my burnout was simply an outlook on life that I needed to change, according to them.

In their mind, I was depressed and just needed to think more positively, look forward to the future and think about other things. I mean, hello? Of course, I *really* wanted to do that. I wanted to move forward very quickly from what had happened and get on with my life.

## Trapped in the Darkness

*But burnout forced me to change who I was. It forced me to see myself differently.*

Those people thought I should just stop thinking about it and move on. These impressions made it that much harder for me and frustrated me, because more than anything in the world, all I wanted was to move on, past this place of isolation that I had found myself trapped in.

I felt totally misunderstood.

I felt people were unsure around me. People were unsure about who this Emma was and how they should deal with her. How should they approach this softer, feebler, more vulnerable, less gregarious, less vivacious, less energetic person?

I must admit, I know it can be tricky to navigate when you come across someone you know has a health issue when you haven't dealt with it yourself before. I too have felt very unsure myself. I think some people feel like they doubt themselves. But here's some advice for those people – just ask them how they are. You shouldn't feel that you should have to know how the other person feels or what they are going through.

For some people, especially at work, I just didn't bother telling them what was going on. It was easier and less of a strain to tell some people. So, I decided that I would only tell people on a need-to-know basis. I only told people that I dealt with a lot at work, and close friends and some of my extended family.

Everyone else just had to suck it up and accept it. Or not. Because not everyone noticed.

Sometimes their ignorance was a blessing! I had bigger problems on my plate and I couldn't burn my precious energy caring about what those people thought. Even though I struggled with their impressions, my main focus and problem was getting through my burnout. Getting through and managing it in the best way I could. And it was a whole new way of being, to put myself first.

My mum had also been through burnout herself. I was lucky that I had her understanding when other people didn't understand. The knowledge of my immediate family, of my mum's burnout – even though it occurred differently to mine – helped bring some awareness within our family. Also, my partner was very understanding. He found a lot of burnout information for me on the web when I was too drained to search for myself. That care, and thoughtfulness made me feel like I was really ok. That I would be ok in the end.

I will always remember that I had his support when I didn't have the support of others. These things gave me strength to get through tough times, when other people were thinking I was depressed or being a bit strange. It's comforting when you have people on your side and it was just so much easier to not have to explain everything to them. They understood a little bit. That was great. It really took some pressure off me.

## Avoid and Carry On

Another thing that that happened incidentally as a result of burnout, was that I just started to avoid things that made me feel uncomfortable and anxious or drained my energy too much. I avoided situations that were too busy, too loud, too noisy or too socially challenging. I retreated away from some work colleagues that I didn't know very well. I realised I couldn't have this huge network of work colleagues anymore. I just had to relate to people in my immediate team and others who I regularly dealt with outside my team. I talked to those people when I needed to, but I didn't put my hand up for public speaking events any more. I didn't do the value-added stuff that I always used to do because I'd changed and I couldn't do it anymore.

I didn't have the energy to spare and I had to look after myself.

I avoided social situations as well. But a result of avoiding things that challenged me, I became more isolated. I became more isolated from my friends and family. It was hard, because being isolated took me away from my support network. I tried to escape what I was going through. But by being on my own most of the time, I thought more, I mulled things over. Again, and again, all the time. And that really didn't help at all.

*I used meditation and relaxing music to chill out. But we're social creatures, we really do need to be around other people. People who are gentle and calm, and who can provide some comfort to a fellow human who's struggling.*

I really, really limited going out for a while or only went places with my partner. Because let's face it, we all have to go out and get a change of scene and perspective at some point. I mean, it was a good feeling to put some nice shoes on, get a little bit dressed up and just go to a café for a big slice of carrot cake – I love the icing! But I learnt which cafes were too noisy, which cafes play the really loud music and I didn't bother going to those ones anymore. It was just too draining and I didn't need that in my life at that time. But in a supportive situation with a person who I loved and trusted, I ventured out in to the world every now and then. This gave me hope that I could carry on and get through this challenge without avoiding everything.

We would go out to a restaurant sometimes or to a market, which I have always enjoyed. It gave me a sense of freedom to be out and about doing something more normal, instead of being trapped at home. Feeling him holding my hand was like a sort of shield from the 'dangers' of the outside world and was a great comfort. I felt so encouraged by his support. All in all, it gave me a sense of normality – a reminder of the old Emma.

## The Need for Care

By and large, I was let down by my managers at work before and after burnout. They didn't accept that I wanted to leave the role that was causing me stress and that I struggled with before burnout – and if I had left before that, maybe it wouldn't have happened. But then once I had burnout, they wanted to pretend it hadn't happened.

I felt my issues were trivialised and put in the 'too hard basket'. The only formal assistance I received was an offer to see the workplace counsellor. It was like I reminded them of their deficiencies, their failure and they didn't want to be confronted by that. I should just stop winging about my work, was the attitude of many male managers. I should simply toughen up a bit and get on with it.

The impression I had from them was, *"Emma, this is life, this is reality. You know, we all have things that we struggle with."*

Well, I thought then and still think that's unfair because in life, some people are more vulnerable than others. Where was the supportive workplace culture, the acceptance of diversity they talked about? Doesn't diversity include accepting all of our different ways of working and our limitations, too? I thought it did. But I lacked support from many of my managers at the time.

After burnout, I changed roles and thankfully got away from shift work – at last! In my new role, my new manager was very supportive of my situation and needs. He simplified my workload by giving me small amounts of work and allowed me to reduce my hours to help me recover. It was nice to feel cared for and supported at last. Without that manager, I would have felt completely isolated and let down by the system that I had given so much of myself to, for many, many years.

During my recovery, the office was getting renovated. I had support from a senior staff member who wasn't my manager. We had loud drilling that seemed to go on for weeks and I couldn't focus. I was feeling more and more agitated trying to concentrate on my work with such loud background noise. Earplugs or headphones just didn't cut it. She allowed me to temporarily set up my workstation in her office and she moved out. This was so incredibly thoughtful and kind of her. She knew what my situation was and I was beyond thankful for that.

The thing that I had to be careful of at work when talking about my issues was the gossip mill. I was cautious about who I told in Human Resources, and who else I told, because I discovered that people like to talk. Things like emails are supposed to be confidential – and really, so are certain conversations. But for some reason, these rules seemed to get pushed aside, which let people like me, down. I felt that some people knew about what happened who I hadn't told, which was unfair and gave me a sense of shame.

I was feeling very vulnerable and insecure about my place at work and where I belonged after burnout. Because I wasn't the same person any more. I felt I wasn't supported by the system that's supposed to be there to support vulnerable people. So, I wondered - who do I go to for support? I was really let down by the culture of gossip.

It was hard for me at work after that.

I was trapped in a dark place with limited people who understood what I was going through.

*All I wanted was for people to care about me or who wanted to understand what I was going through, so I didn't feel alone.*

I went into the workplace after university with the belief that to succeed in my life and career, you just had to give and give and give some more. Push through, do overtime, attain that deadline.

It's not right and its unsustainable.

Eventually, I gave myself the care and support I needed. Learning about mindfulness meditation was a way that I could calm myself on the inside, even when there was turmoil outside. So, when I came across managers that didn't want to really understand what I was going through or the work gossip mill or simply harsh background noise, I could use mindfulness tools to focus on myself, my breathing and momentarily escape the unbearable stressors in my life.

When we focus on the breath while meditating, we can let go and accept the things that don't serve us, that don't help or support us. And regain a sense of serenity again.

One quick technique I learnt was to put one hand on my heart and the other on my tummy and start focusing in on my breathing. I would inhale to the count of four and exhale much more slowly to the count of eight. I could do this anywhere, in the car, the office or at home.

If I was at home, I would light a scented candle and find a peaceful spot in the sun, to release the stress of all that had happened. As time went on, I included this practice more and more regularly whenever I started to feel the tell-tale tightness in my face.

To keep pushing yourself continually, without adequate down time, is not a way to succeed in life. The way to succeed in life is to realise your limitations. You're going to be good at some things. You're going to succeed at those, but you're not going to be good at everything. And that's okay. In the end, you shouldn't push and force yourself to succeed based on the expectations of others, because you might start to believe them yourself.

And there's a chance you will come undone. Just like I did.

## Chapter Four

# The Stress of STEMM

*"The greatest weapon against stress is our ability to choose one thought over another."*

(William James)

I had been working in the STEMM field when I was affected by burnout. I'd worked with the same organisation for over 15 years, in various roles. I enjoyed my work and gave a lot to whatever I was working on. But in the end, that way of working and constantly giving, was unsustainable for me. I was under a lot of stress. I could no-longer manage the incessant and varied workload, and expectation to continuously achieve results and high-profile outcomes. Eventually, it took a toll on me. The high demands of work, after-hours work, plus the pressure to maintain such a high level of performance in a competitive, male-dominated environment, I believe all contributed to the stress I felt, and my burnout.

## Information Overload

It all really started when I was at university. That's where I learnt to deal with multiple tasks. I was doing all that was required of any university student striving for a degree, including; field work, detailed assignments, field reports and laboratory practicals. As well as my studies, I was tutoring first and second year students, so I could have an income. I was go-go-go and thriving on all this activity – feeling stimulated and happy to be succeeding. But the trouble is, this continues into your professional life once you get a job after university.

There is a constant need to succeed at all costs.

Succeed in the marks you get, succeed in the day-to-day management of your studies. But there is not one mention that you need to manage your wellbeing and balance your life. There is not one mention (that I can recall) of making students aware of the importance of taking time out for a break. The need to balance work and play with down time.

I believe this is really important, as it all starts here. It's where people can establish good or bad habits.

There were so many multiple tasks that I needed to achieve when I first got a position after university. In those early days, I needed to make a good impression on my manager, so I always put my hand up for more work opportunities. I had to keep up to the day-to-day work of report writing, data collation in spreadsheets and data analysis, as well as the weekly meetings, team briefs and emails to read and reply to.

*There was a lot to adjust to as a fledgling professional and I was so eager to please and do well. But I later realized that in doing this, I was giving a lot of my energy away.*

Giving a lot of my energy away on one thing is no good for anyone, because there's no balance. But that's what I was doing. It didn't seem to slow down at all as there were opportunities for field work, which was the best part of the job and why I went to university in the first place.

I loved going to new places around Australia, places off the beaten track. But when we came back to work, there was always so much to catch up on. There was travel admin to do as well as get samples analysed, start to work on the data and write up the results. A lot of research was also needed, which, at the time, I really enjoyed. It was fun discovering new things, different theories and approaches.

I attended conferences when the opportunity arose, which always meant a lot of preparation. If I was presenting, I had to prepare a slide presentation for that timeslot and practice the presentation beforehand and gather feedback – then make changes if necessary. This was fun for a while. It's enlivening, it's invigorating, when you're at the forefront of new research.

You're talking to experts from around the world and interacting with those people at conferences. And when you have visiting scientists who want to see your work, it's such a great thing to be a part of – especially when there's all this new work happening that can help solve real problems that we face in our society.

Conferences were the type of value-added task that I found really added to the existing tasks and the mounting workload that we were required to manage. There was a lot of independent work, managing your own tasks and workload but it was nice to be left to make progress myself. Despite that, our managers didn't check to see how we were truly handling everything, that wasn't their mandate. It was rather to check that you were meeting your deadlines and making progress towards project goals.

It was up to you to speak up and say no, it wasn't working.

This depends on so many things, but in particular, it depends on your manager and your personality. For me, I didn't naturally feel I could speak up and say no or say I needed help to balance things with most of my managers. Unless I had support from colleagues, I wouldn't really ever speak up. I would just try to manage it all, but this led to mounting stress and imbalance in my life, which wasn't balanced with down-time to relax and recuperate. It was only later in my career that I became more confident in my needs.

There were times when thinking about dealing with co-workers and managers ended up being so draining on my energy that it took the focus away from my work. I became anxious about certain colleagues I didn't get on with and didn't know how to get past these kinds of obstacles.

At the time, I wasn't open to seeing a counsellor or coach to assist with these challenges. I think the stress of managing relationships at work became overwhelming and took a toll on me. In particular, after I had burnout, everything was harder for me at work. Workplace relationships were something I started to avoid or not deal with, which added to a lack of enjoyment of my work and the organisation I worked for.

## High Achievers Galore

The STEMM field is a place of high-achievers galore. You're working alongside people who have done wonderful work and have achieved amazing things and you can't help but want to be up there in the spotlight with those people.

It really appeals to your ego, to be part of this high achiever's club.

To be a glory hunter, to be in the spotlight, to do media interviews about your own work. There are so many self-promotion and career-making opportunities available. If you're the type of person who seeks out those opportunities, they are there for the taking if you have the time, willingness and ability. If you have that personality that wants to do it, you can achieve those amazing things. It's great fun to be a part of it – to deliver good, helpful information to people who need it.

But then alongside that, there comes a lot of pressure. There's pressure to get more qualifications, to study for a Masters or a PhD – or even go on and do a post-doctorate if you want. I had worked alongside so many others who had achieved these things.

There's also pressure to aspire to be a manager. Since I first started working, there's management courses that you do as a young employee or graduate and you can't help but think that one day you will make it as a manager. But management roles aren't for everyone – in reality they are very limited. So, you have to be an extra special person with extra special skills (and probably a workaholic!) to fill one of those positions.

It took many years for me to see through the bullshit and not be fooled by these expectations.

I was certainly not cut out for management. I wasn't a workaholic and needed time to myself away from my career and the ever-present work 'stuff' that filled my mind. Some of my colleagues lived and breathed the work they did. Its lovely to have such a passion for the work, but there also needs to be balance.

# The Stress of STEMM

*I think I put pressure on myself to achieve, achieve, achieve, to keep up with the frantic pace of what other colleagues were doing.*

I thought I was doing it for my own career and convinced myself of that, but there was a competitive culture to succeed at play, too. I committed myself to a professional society, to work on the committee, thinking I might be able to gain some credibility or recognition from colleagues. It might be handy on my resume, I remember thinking. It wasn't something that I usually did in work hours – no, it was something that I did on top of my normal work.

I think this really put extra pressure on me as I was not balancing work with me-time and wasn't getting enough time to relax.

I would contribute to other groups like the Diversity committee and the Woman's Network, which were really valuable things to be part of. But I think these extra activities put pressure on me and gave me less down time to wind down from my work role. I was doing too much and as I was thinking about similar things to my main role, I just wasn't having enough down-time to free my mind of work topics. If I could have been less analytical and more creative in my spare time, perhaps I could have achieved more balance.

Another thing that we were expected to do after hours was read articles. Read the latest research in the area that we were writing a report on, because you might not have time to do that sort of stuff during work hours. Unfortunately, you're expected to write research articles after work, because there often wasn't time to do this sort of stuff during work hours.

Basically, how I performed came down to the expectations of my manager.

I believe that when you have a high-achieving manager who expects a lot from their staff because they also commit a lot of extra time to work themselves, can lead to increased stress and overwork. I mean, if you have a manager who works late and has an unspoken rule that their staff also work extra hours, it's unfair to expect them to stay and continue to work when they are due to finish. For example, I know of people who didn't leave work until the manager left at the end of the day. They'll say it doesn't happen, but it depends on your relationship to that manager, what stage of career you're at and the type of personality you have.

For example, if you're the type of person to stick up for yourself, or you don't care what others think, then this probably wouldn't happen to you. But if you're the opposite of that, quietly spoken and eager to please, then you're more likely to stay and keep up appearances with a manager who's working late. Over the long term, I believe this way of working, leads to increased stress and a lack of work-life balance.

## The Burning Woman

When I was working in the middle of this amazing career, I didn't allow myself the time I needed to wind down and I started to gradually burn down. It's like I started to turn into a woman who was once on fire burning brightly to burning down and eventually getting snuffed out.

There were so many demands in this role.

*As a woman working in a male-dominated field, I felt there was a need to constantly prove myself.*

As a woman, you need to keep up the good work, maintain the highest standards and never let your guard down. Just keep up the achieving and proving and constantly giving.

But I couldn't do that forever. I couldn't do that day in and day out without it taking a toll.

I was also an introverted person who was really required to be extroverted at work in order to get the work done. To communicate adequately with others, at meetings and in presentations, I felt I had to develop an extrovert's personality in those situations. A lot of scientists aren't extroverts. But they love the work and do the extra things anyway. But there might not be as much pressure on employees if you just had to do the work and focus on the core work that you're employed to do.

So many things are expected of a professional in STEMM.

You're expected to have interpersonal skills to liaise with stakeholders both internally and externally – you might need to acquire some data sets from an external organization, and so are expected to liaise with them by email or phone calls. This stuff takes time and energy.

If a high-level manager required some advice on an aspect of the work that you're working on, then you need to drop what you're doing and provide that information.

To work collaboratively in a team, but also work independently requires a certain flexibility of personality to be able to do so. Looking back, I think I was constantly adapting my brain to operate in these different modes. All this involves preparation, of course, taking you away from that core work that you're expected to keep up with.

There's often conflicting or competing priorities, which they're open about. I mean, often it's described in the selection criteria for a role. You're expected to manage competing priorities and tasks yourself, whether it be getting a report done and at the same time as preparing a presentation. There's always a justification for it but all of a sudden, you have got extra work to do that wasn't initially planned for.

So again, I needed to adapt my sphere of thinking and manage my time in an ever-decreasing timeframe. I think these additional tasks had an impact and could be quite stressful on me. The pressure of deadlines was always there, which over time, I started to not manage very well.

## The Stress of STEMM

*I thought I absorbed stress ok. However, I think that all I really did was to push it down and hide it outwardly – while inwardly, I was building up stress like a volcano builds up pressure before it explodes.*

When that started to happen, I was on the road to becoming the burning woman. While it's said that the additional tasks don't come without an impact, I believe my burnout is evidence that they do.

Overall, I think being in an analytical role took a huge toll on me personally, because I didn't give myself any time to be creative. I could have been doing something creative in my spare time, but I felt I didn't have the mental space for it because my brain was at full capacity from being in an analytical mode all day. So, I just needed to recuperate from that type of work at the end of a work day. So, I would go to the gym, have a drink and eat yummy food. They felt like the necessities of life then as I was so brain dead at the end of a work day. Every now and then, I'd have a bath to relax, but not often enough to establish a good habit.

For me now, I love to do art therapy and colouring in books when I can. Colouring encourages me to focus on one thing and enjoy the picture coming to life as I work. I ensure that I don't rush or put any pressure on myself to 'achieve' anything fantastic. It doesn't have to be the 'best' creation, just one that I can work on in a gentle, mindful way. I enjoy choosing my colour palette and focusing in on the colour of the flower petals, stamens and leaves, or the intricate details of a mandala. It's a wonderful way to be still and calm.

I have also taken up more gardening, because being outside in nature is a great way for me to recharge. I have my vegetable patch, where I like to plant zucchinis, beetroot, snow peas and pumpkins. Then there's my green space, that I have filled with a combination of hardy native and more European type plants. I feel great if I have spent a bit of time in the garden every day. To get the oxygen pumping around the body and some Vitamin D is like an antidote to all the pressures of life.

At heart, I'm a creative person and being in an analytical role – doing analysis as the primary part of my job and then also doing those things after hours as well – really put a strain on my brain, which contributed to my burnout.

Therefore, I intend on doing more creative things in the future. I hope you can find a way to incorporate this into your own life too, and create more balance.

## Chapter Five

# Burnout Mama Life

*"Peace. It does not mean to be in a place where there is no noise, trouble or hard work. It means to be in the midst of those things and still be calm in your heart."*
(Unknown)

After our baby boy was born, I wholeheartedly felt what an amazing blessing he was. Looking at the wonderful bundle of joy who was born into our world, the love hormones kept me going on a maternal high for a few weeks initially. But after that, it became more about settling into a pretty chaotic routine that was always moving in unexpected directions. I didn't ever feel like I could relax in this new crazy space of motherhood, but instead I had to constantly adapt and change with my baby. This made me feel uncomfortable and uncertain.

I usually felt as if my world was sliding in a direction that I had no say in or control over.

For someone with burnout, the huge expectations placed on a mama were not easy to manage. It was a really hard position to find myself in, to suddenly be the bearer of this 'motherload.' Although my partner assisted in many ways, the mental load and stress that it put on me as a new mama with burnout led to many days in tears, not coping well, not surviving and not getting through all that was required of me.

## Baby Blues

In the months after the birth, I went through a lot of emotional upheavals. This was my first baby and as with a lot of new mamas, everything is scary and new. I wanted to do it just right, which caused me to worry a lot.

It was during this time that I discovered I was dealing with postnatal anxiety.

This was a combination of the hormonal changes I experienced during the pregnancy and also finding out that I had a low-lying placenta. This complication was an added stressor for me that I needed to keep a close eye on and attend extra appointments for.

It all turned out fine in the end.

But after the baby came, there were more hormonal changes and I had some breastfeeding issues, which meant that after six months, I gave up breastfeeding altogether due to infection. It was very, very painful at the time and caused me a lot of stress and worry. So, once I got through the ordeal of having to stop breastfeeding quickly – with all the leaks and swollen lumps – I was happy to see the end of it. I wasn't that keen on breastfeeding anyway, with all the 'breast management' that was needed. I readily gave it up for bottle feeding, which thankfully my son took to with gusto.

Another thing that added to my anxiety was the isolation that I felt being at home long days with a baby. This was especially hard after having a sleep deprived, restless night – combined with the fact that our family don't live nearby. There was family help, but it was about two or three hours away. My mum used to come up and stay for a few nights to help out, but then I was on my own again.

I valued that time immensely, but it was never enough.

I didn't have a reliable person that I could call on. For example, if I was struggling one afternoon or one morning, it was just us to handle it. I'd also had two close friends who recently left and this made it hard because up until that point, while I was pregnant, I had friends living close by. Then later in the pregnancy, they left. One, due to work commitments and the other wanting to relocate for a different lifestyle.

It was really hard just not having people that I could call on when I needed that help.

They were only a phone call away, but there's nothing like getting a cuddle from a close friend when you're feeling alone or in need of some extra support.

One of the regular things that I did to overcome my sense of isolation as a new mama was a mother's group that formed from a wonderful course I did called *'Calm Parenting'* (now Transform Parenting, Appendix A) for parents and mamas.

It started as a weekly meeting, one morning a week, to learn about what we were going through as new mamas. It was wonderful and so beneficial that I found this group, where I could talk through things with like-minded mamas.

After the course finished, we kept in touch and met once a week at a cafe when our babies were small. It was a lovely way for me to get out of the house and just be with other mums. But it caused me a lot of stress and anxiety, being with people that I didn't know very well.

I didn't feel comfortable with them yet, but at the same time I needed them. Weird, huh?

Although it was tricky, I pushed through my fears because it gave me a little escape and positive boost from the world at home.

The other thing that really added to my anxiety, which every new mama experiences, is that I had little to no time to myself. There's little me-time, little time for self-care. Some days, when the baby was young, I sometimes forgot to brush my teeth or didn't have time to shower. I was so immersed in the needs of the baby that I forgot what my own needs were.

It's so important to give yourself time to include those basic things.

Even just sitting and looking out the window, listening to the birds with a quiet cup of tea was a challenge. So, there were times when I just left the pile of dishes, the washing, the never-ending tidying and checking the baby, and rested. I did those calm things and left the jobs when I was feeling frantic and wound up and trapped.

*It was so important to just have some quiet time to myself. Although this was difficult when my mind was in over-drive – always thinking, planning ahead and checking if the baby was ok.*

One of the main things that played on my mind was, is he sleeping well? My son had reflux problems and a lot of wind, which would disturb his sleep. If it got really uncomfortable and painful, he would wake up crying, so I would need to pick him up and pat his back to help digestion. But it was confusing because you're not supposed to pick a baby up if they are crying when they rouse from sleep.

It was stressful and hard to know what's right, when you're totally new at it.

I found a psychologist, who I had an emergency consultation with when my child was about six months old. This was a great relief to me as I was not going well. I had issues with my breasts at the time and was in a lot of pain as well as dealing with everything on not much sleep, which played havoc with my sense of calm.

The psychologist helped me to find a way forward, so I could better navigate this disarray and crazy place I found myself in. Finding a name that I could call this whirling mix of emotions and feelings that I had coursing through me was kind of nice. It gave me some understanding of what I was going through. Something I could Google and find more out about, to help myself.

One of the biggest calming things that gave me some relief was the deep breathing exercises.

Deep breathing helped calm my racing heart and slow me down. My psychologist said what was happening was I would start the day at a heightened level.

When I was thinking about everything I needed to do in the early hours of the day, my mind was racing as I began the day. It probably even started sometime during the night, because when I would wake to breastfeed, I was instantly on alert.

By the time morning came, I was instantly thinking about how to solve this issue or how to deal with that issue.

Often when I was sleep deprived, I was starting the day in a hyper vigilant state. So as the day went on, my levels of stress and anxiety would increase from there. If I was never given my chance to wind down, it would keep escalating and getting worse.

*One of the most valuable things that she taught me was to set yourself up for the day by doing some meditation and calm breathing.*

So, although it was hard, I would try to put aside some time during the morning either after the first feed or during the morning nap – when he was young – to do some deep breathing exercises.

Similar to the mindfulness meditation, but simpler, I would just have to try and focus on the breath by breathing in through the nose while counting, then breath out through the mouth as slowly as I could while counting. The counting gives the active mind something to focus on, away from the anxieties and concerns of the day. It was so hard to do at first as I was overly anxious and tense, but over time, I started to focus more on my breath.

It usually had a calming effect for an hour or if I was lucky, two hours, before the usual stress of mothering got to me again. Plus, it was hard to implement a new habit, with all the chaos and challenges a new mama faces. But not only was it calming and healthy for my body, I felt as if I was doing something for myself, which had a positive effect on days when there was no extra time to dedicate to breathing exercises.

## Accepting Discomfort and Chaos

When you're a person who is used to slightly more order and have the ability to plan and forecast what's happening, it's pretty challenging to let all that go when you become a mama. Basically, having a baby is pretty chaotic. There's a lot of upheaval. There are changes to feeding patterns, sleeping patterns, teething – there's so many different phases they go through, which requires the parents to have the ability to adapt quickly to small changes as they come up.

I found this very, very challenging and it often caused me to feel upset with myself for not being able to do what I thought a mother should be able to do. I felt this all-encompassing guilt. It was so hard to adapt, especially when I was tired and functioning on much less sleep than I was used to. When, as new parents you are trying to establish good sleeping patterns, it takes so much energy.

I couldn't accept that I didn't have control over these things.

I found that a lot about being a mama and being a parent is just being able to accept the changes that you're dealt. Being able to accept each new phase that your child goes through. But having anxiety meant that all the small changes that the baby was going through really stressed me out. It was a big, big change for me to be able to start to realise that I had to accept that I didn't have control over those things.

When I was feeling rushed, I felt like I was always trying to catch up. I know that I wouldn't be the only person who experienced this. But things like remembering what goes into the baby bag when you're going out; wipes, tissues, nappies, snacks, a toy, etc. There was a lot of stuff to remember in the early days.

I always felt like I was running back inside from the car just before I was leaving to put those last few things in. I felt disorganised and playing catch up, when I'd always been a fairly organised person. It made me realise how much simpler life was before kids.

Part of the adjustment and part of the accepting of discomfort, is accepting that the personal changes you go through as a woman and new mama. There's a massive shift in our identity. As well as adapting to all the practical things of a new mama, we have to grapple with who we were, compared to who we are now. There's a lot going on during those early months and years after you have a child. There's so much we aren't yet comfortable with, but we have to find a way through it anyway. However messy and uncomfortable it is, we have to accept and come to terms with disorder and keep going.

It's a time I will never forget because it changed me deeply.

A couple of years later, I learnt about the changes mamas go through in the early stages of motherhood, are common to many new mamas. It has a name – *matrescence* (Taylor-Kabbaz, 2019). Instead of feeling like I was alone going through all those changes, if I had known earlier about matrescence, it would have helped me get through it a lot easier.

All we need is to talk more openly about what we are going through as new mamas, to break down the unreasonable expectations we have of ourselves and from others. If we talk more to demystify stigmas about how society views mamas, hopefully it will help mamas of the future to get through this time of upheaval with less struggle and more support.

**Burnout Mama**

Burnout happened two years before I had the baby. Which meant, there really wasn't enough time for me to fully recover before becoming immersed in another big challenge. I'd recovered a little bit and made some progress from burnout before the baby, but I was still really learning about my burnout, trying to make personal changes.

So, when the baby came, I was still trying to pull back from being too busy. This is really, really difficult when you have a baby. Mamas are always tired and busy, and for someone with burnout, it was especially hard to be in that space.

I just wanted to stop.

I just wanted to relax and have some space to myself. But you don't have that luxury.

*Being burnt out, I just found that I had less energy and less stamina to pull myself through the challenging nights of sleep deprivation.*

That's where my husband really, really came to the fore and helped me so much. To this day, he still helps me with the nights when our child is restless, sick or has nightmares. Because it's so hard for me to be tired and function without feeling like I'm imploding. Like I'm losing my stability, sense of calm and what grounds me.

A big part of my ability to cope and pull through each day as a mama, was getting enough sleep. I really needed my sleep as everyone does, but the trouble with me was that I was still recovering from burnout, managing my relaxation and ability to wind down.

Many times, I was so wound up from being in this hypervigilant state throughout the day, I often couldn't relax to sleep at the end of the day. Back then, I was probably getting to sleep by midnight or one o'clock after a really busy day and still had to be able to function the next day.

When I didn't have enough breaks or rests during the day, I would be so wound up after doing dinner, and then the bath and bedtime routine. Even when he was a baby, our son wasn't one to go to sleep early. He wasn't ready for bed until eight or nine o'clock at night, which made it hard to adequately wind down enough before I went to bed at the end of the day.

We would both be so tired, me from the day at home as an anxious mum and my husband from work, entertaining our son with books to establish a bedtime routine. Sometimes after breastfeeding during the night, I couldn't get back to sleep. I would feel wound up and anxious and other times, it felt like insomnia and I was getting into a bad sleep pattern from waking up so much at night. It was such a relief and blessing when he got to just one feed a night. That was much easier on me, as I could manage one baby-related disruption to my sleep.

Overall, I didn't have any relaxation techniques fully established by the time I had the baby. So here I was, trying to learn about motherhood, what the baby's needs were, what I needed as a mama, as well as negotiating with my husband. Then at the same time, I was learning about what I needed to do to relax adequately and find time to do that. It really was a big, messy, melting pot for me as a burnt-out mama.

*I often thought to myself, "I don't know how mamas do it. I don't know how other mamas survive with two or even three kids. How can they bear the burden of the emotional load we have to contend with as a mama, without health impacts, psychological impacts and relationship impacts?"*

This motherload created tension and conflict between my partner and I, as I could not see why I should always be the bearer of so many hidden tasks and expectations. I couldn't accept this workload and pushed back against it. I think I was resisting burnout again, or felt the real threat of it.

The challenge is absorbing the stress and not letting it overwhelm and dominate. Because when we don't, the result is unhealthy eating and drinking or yelling at our children and spouses to release the stress and emotional tension.

My poor husband took on a lot more than other dads would have. I thank him for that.

I recognise that it's taken a toll on him and both of us to get through the early childhood years. But we are doing it, we are getting through it. Even with all the obstacles of being a mama with burnout.

Burnout is always there, never far away as a reminder that I need to slow down and be still as often as I can.

This is a recent example of my reality and how I can juggle the many tasks required of a mama. It's a little peek into my life on one busy afternoon and how I got through it:

"I had a productive day editing my book chapters and was feeling great as I'd completed a chapter and part of another. But that afternoon, I had to get some groceries on the way to a meeting with a childcare educator, then pick up my son afterwards. The shopping went ok, but I ended up buying more than I intended to, so I overdid it there. Then I didn't have much time to rest in the car before I drove 10 minutes over to the childcare centre. Once there, I did some breathing in the car, felt a little bit wound up, but externally, I seemed to be going ok. Although, I knew deep within myself that I was going to suffer later. Then I had a half hour discussion with the educator, which was fine but I started to get hot and uncomfortable in the room as I didn't have any water with me. Then I picked up my son, who was also tired and wound up from a busy day, so didn't sit in his car seat very easily. Then I got home, unpacked the shopping, then the dishwasher, then gave myself a 10-minute break before starting dinner. Phew!"

This was a hectic afternoon for me and ended up making me feel tense and irritable. This is the type of task upon task activity that stresses me, especially when I don't have enough time to adequately wind down in between each task. That night, it was hard for me to slow down and relax for sleeping, plus my meditation didn't go well as I was unfocused. Then I had a slightly more restless sleep and the following day, I felt tired and less capable of being productive. I needed more rest time, and thankfully I could give it to myself as my son was at day care.

I call this a classic-Emma-burnout-scenario that still crops up when I don't – or simply can't – manage my workload. I'm sure others who don't suffer from burnout would recover a lot quicker. But for me, one busy afternoon leaves its mark until later that night and sometimes into the next day.

The life of a burnout mama certainly isn't without its challenges.

I created an inspirational note for myself, somewhere in the midst of being a new mama, which I stuck on my bedroom wall. It was just across from my pillow, so that when I woke up in the morning, I could read it and set myself up for the day in a positive way. I knew I was struggling and felt frustrated with myself and how I was handling the crazy new world of motherhood. So, I tried to create something meaningful that would help me change my thinking a bit.

The note said:

*"Tomorrow is a fresh new day.*

*Trust these burnout symptoms will pass.*

*I am grateful for... today."*

In a small way, it did help me get through tough times, when I doubted myself and when anxiety dominated my thinking. This may provide some inspiration – to create your own note to help you get through tough times.

## *Chapter Six*

# The 2020 Cauldron

*"Your calm mind is the ultimate weapon against your challenges."*
(Bryant McGill)

2020 was like a cauldron; a pressure-cooker type of year that led to increased stress levels for me. I know 2020 was hard for many living in the midst of a global pandemic – and this is what I went through. It was a volatile mix of stress that all started with smoke from bushfires and dealing with the trauma of the fires as they threatened family.

With everyone at home during lockdown, there was increased pressure on me as a professional and mama, with added expectations and responsibilities. I was giving too much of my energy and time to others, day in day out, leaving very little time for myself. There was hardly any balance between work and home, which left minimal rest and recovery time. What this meant was the start of me really saying no to things that weren't good for me, noticing what I needed, and acting on it. It was the year that almost pushed me over the edge into another cycle of burnout.

## Real Inferno Trigger

There were many triggers in 2020 and the first was the bushfire inferno that started in the Currowan State Forest, east of Canberra. For us living on the east coast, it all started with smoke from fires that took off at the end of 2019 and continued into 2020.

We had smoke in Canberra for days on end.

There was smoke around in the morning that might lift during the day as the wind picked up. But then in the evening, the smoke seemed to creep inland over the hills from the east. We had to race around and close all the windows before the smoke hit in the evening. I'd go up into the backyard after dinner and check to see if there was any smoke coming. Some mornings, you'd wake up to smoke, and other mornings it was clear – those days were a real blessing. A fresh relief from the toxic air we had to breathe and lookout for. We were ever-vigilant to changing weather conditions, wind directions and air quality.

## The 2020 Cauldron

It was hot that summer and we couldn't have the air conditioner on as it needed replacing, but we couldn't open the windows either due to smoke. There was not much time to be outside with a small child, which was really hard to keep activities going inside. We did crafts, played with blocks and did hide and seek, over and over again. We just had to take advantage of mornings or a few hours during the day when the wind blew the smoke away and the air was fresh.

If we didn't have that, we would have gone mad.

For us adults, we started wearing face-masks at the start of 2020. Not because of the coronavirus yet, but because of the smoke. Our son was too small to wear a mask, they wouldn't fit young kids well and it was a toxic place to be. Air quality was deemed hazardous and way above what was thought safe for people to breathe. We often checked the *Air Matters* app to see how far above normal and how hazardous it was.

It was an unbelievable situation to live through, especially when we were all so used to fresh air. I mean Canberra wasn't a place where we got smog or anything like that. We were stressed out and on edge, concerned for the welfare of our young son. We purchased an air purifier, which helped clean the air inside our house, but it's amazing how much smoke can infiltrate the window and door frames.

Before going outside, we always checked the air quality and would check it repetitively throughout the day. It was a terrible place to be. We were really concerned for the health of our young child. We were asking ourselves if there would be any lasting impacts on his health. We didn't know. Because the fires were unprecedented, no-one did.

My parents, who live near Moruya on the south coast, were also under threat from the bushfires. We stayed with them for Christmas in 2019. Some days we had light smoke in the air, other days it was a bit heavier or we could see the dark smoke column in the sky to the north. But down on the coast, we were thankful for the sea breeze to freshen the air but felt on high alert if it got too strong.

After Christmas, we just made it back to Canberra before they shut the Princes Highway – I believe it happened that afternoon. The Kings Highway was shut up Clyde Mountain because of the Currowan fire, so we had to go the long way up Brown Mountain via Cooma. At one stage, once we made it up the range before Nimmitabel, we were driving past a massive column of smoke to the north east.

It was really scary.

It seemed there was fires popping up all around us and checking the *Fires Near Me* app on the way, grass fires seemed to be appearing quickly next to the Princes highway. I think we got back home in the nick of time. But the smoke was thick in Canberra and we just didn't want to be there. It felt like we were trapped by smoke and fire, like there was nowhere safe for us to escape to.

It was a toxic environment for our health and for the health of our child.

# The 2020 Cauldron

*I found out that inhaling smoke triggers a fight or flight response. As humans, we are hard-wired to run from danger, and smoke is one of the triggers. We were living with that feeling every day, as were so many who endured the fires.*

After we got home, all I wanted to do was unpack the car and sort through the Christmas presents. But we also wanted to escape and get out of town. It was like we were acting on that fight or flight response. We we're looking at all our options and considered either flying to Tasmania or going north to Queensland.

But in the end, we thought we would drive to Wollongong where we'd be north of the worst of the smoke that was coming from the South Coast fires. So that's what we did, we drove up the Hume Highway, always checking the news and I remember we didn't even stop for lunch. I got in the back seat and fed my son lunch, so we didn't have to stop.

We stayed there for a week or so. It was a blessing to be at the coast where there was only a little bit of smoke around. It was nowhere near as thick as it had been in Canberra, because the sea breeze always moved it away. The place we stayed at had fire refugees staying there who were from the South Coast.

In the carpark, we noticed one couple had their car really loaded up and their dog with them. Wollongong was a respite for us, but the news was full of updates and images of the fires. Plus, I was worried about my parents who were still in the midst of it and under threat of fire.

Then, my parents were at risk of bushfire impact in Moruya. Due to the wind direction, the fire was forecast to hit Batemans Bay and parts of the South Coast on New Year's Eve. Mum and dad were packing up treasured things, photos and heirlooms, and preparing their house for ember attack and bushfire.

The lack of phone reception meant it was hard for them to get updates and hard to find out how they were. They used the radio when they had power, and I conveyed messages and screenshots of fire maps and wind directions, hoping they could charge their phones and see my messages before the fire came. It was so stressful and scary, knowing what was coming and that they may or may not have access to the information.

In the end, for them it got too dangerous to stay at home as the town water supply wasn't working to give the firefighters priority to the water. They felt they couldn't fight a fire if it arrived on their doorstep without enough water pressure. So, they gladly moved to the Moruya Showgrounds for a few nights in their camper van, along with many other locals and holiday-makers.

I felt such a sense of relief knowing they were at the showgrounds. I thought; at least they could get up-to-date information from officials there and had a buffer of grass surrounding them. But every night I went to bed late, checking the latest updates on the weather and then would have a restless few hours sleep before I woke up to check my phone for news again. It was a worrying time for all my family. The not knowing, the waiting, the wondering. My anxious mind was doing its best to fill in the gaps when there wasn't information, which meant I wasn't calm. It wasn't a good way to live for an extended period of time. At all.

## The COVID-19 Wakeup Call

Then coronavirus hit, turning the world as we knew it upside down. It was yet another pressure that we had to contend with in 2020. Following the fires my heart rate and stress response was already high. In addition, in January I had started a new job, which was an added stressor. I had just started adjusting to my new role and team, and then by March, we were thrown into a new way of doing things - working from home, with Zoom meetings and check-ins from our manager to make sure we were working.

So, I was going through a big adjustment to a new job, a new scenario of working from home and the pressures that went with that. I was working three days a week at that time. At home, we didn't have a separate room or a study that I could use to work. I was basically in the dining area, with a toddler at home and my husband was also working from home. The lines between work and home were completely blurred, which made it so hard to be in that space without taking on stress.

We were in lockdown and my husband started shopping for supplies as he wanted to be prepared for the worst-case scenario. We bought into the toilet paper fiasco and had only used up all of our toilet paper from that in mid-2021! He wanted to purchase a freezer to store extra food, so we didn't have to leave the house if the coronavirus started to get really bad in Australia. Thankfully, it didn't. But we couldn't find a freezer in Canberra as they were all sold out. We found one online in Nowra, which we ended up buying.

One day, my husband hooked up the trailer and travelled to Nowra and back just to get the freezer – which turned out to be the size of a fridge! Then we started buying bulk quantities of meat and frozen veggies. It was a little silly and really contributed to my ever-increasing stress levels.

So here I was, working from home, packing away our tinned food and freezing perishable food supplies, while also managing a toddler. We decided to take our son out of day care so we could all be together, safely at home. I was trying to make progress on my work and focus on a report I was writing at the time, to make a positive impact in my new role. I was doing this in between toilet training, cleaning up mess that was always there and meal preparation.

My working from home routine looked something like this; I would do some work in the morning before morning tea, then I would get up to make morning tea and then get back to work before lunch and repeat the routine over and over. There might've been a meeting on zoom I had to attend. I found my head was in so many places and trying to focus with all this new background noise was super draining for me.

I felt overwhelmed and frantic trying to meet the needs of everyone.

## The 2020 Cauldron

*I was giving too much to everyone but myself. We had a toddler who couldn't be left alone for more than one or two minutes at a time.*

Luckily, my husband's job at the time allowed him some flexibility and he could take our son out of the house for part of the afternoon, at least. This strange new topsy-turvy place we found ourselves in, took a massive, massive toll on me and on all of us as a family.

But it was the wake-up call I needed.

### No! Not That Again

I didn't have the stamina or ability to shoulder the stress and extra pressures of working from home. Due to my previous experience of burnout, I was prone to overwhelm and exhaustion. After a couple of months working from home, I started to feel like I did when I first had burnout. I started to feel unsettled, jittery and kind of shaky in my mind.

At first my thoughts were racing, thinking about so many different things. Then I couldn't focus on anything very well at all. I started to get anxious about those feelings because I didn't want to go through burnout again.

Then, something in me lit up.

*I was being pushed to my limits and I knew I couldn't go through that again. Coronavirus awakened me to the reality I was facing.*

I had a child now and I couldn't risk my health again when I had the responsibility of looking after my family too. So, after chatting with my husband, we realised that we could shoulder the financial situation if I left my job. It was a wonderful feeling to think there was a way out for me. This was a big turning point and where I started to say no to things that weren't good for me.

After a brief chat with my manager, I went on leave. I knew I had to stop work straight away. I was stressed and not coping well. I had sick leave owing and saw my doctor, where I got a medical certificate. A few weeks off work gave me space to get some sort of normality into my health again. I started to feel a bit more settled and could think about what I needed to do.

I knew what I needed to do this time.

I gave in my notice and left the job. I went into the office and packed up my desk. It was empty as everyone was working from home. It felt quite eerie going back there. I didn't say many goodbyes as there was no-one in the office for a farewell. But I saw a couple of people. I had coffee with my old managers and was glad to do that as they helped me when I came back to work after my initial burnout. Then, I happily packed up my desk and loaded some things into the car.

I started to focus on me, the essentials in my life and my family.

I was ready to finish up and just be at home and leave all the stress and hassles behind. Finally, I was ready. I didn't want to go through burnout again. It was a good feeling. I said no and there was no doubt in my mind.

I knew this was the right decision.

Having already been through burnout, I was so sure about how I felt this time. I knew I'd reached my limits. I didn't let the self-talk about finances, work entitlements and career, confuse and jumble my mind about what I did and didn't need. I knew what I didn't need in my life and that was stress and overwhelm. Plus, this time, I had the support of a loving husband by my side to get me over the line. I wasn't on my own with payment responsibilities and didn't have to hack it all alone. The clincher was our son, who always demanded so much of me that I couldn't risk letting myself sink into a mire of overwhelm again. That would be too much for the family, for everyone. So, I bravely stepped up, and loudly and defiantly said, *"NO! I'm not doing that again."*

Thanks to what I learned from my first bout of burnout, I made it through 2020 in one piece –just.

## *Chapter Seven*

# Unlocking Life's Lessons

*"Awareness is like the sun. When it shines on things, they are transformed."*

(Thich Nhat Hanh)

One of the hardest things about recovering from burnout – whatever form of burnout you might have – is the self-acceptance of what's happened. Acceptance is one of the biggest lessons I've learnt. Once I had unlocked that, my outlook and perspective changed and I started to move forward again.

I could start planning for the future and start living life anew.

All I wanted was to live my life, again. I found it super hard to accept my burnout because it meant I had to change. It was really hard to change because I felt that I wasn't going to be me anymore – and if I was going to change, who was Emma? That's what I asked myself.

But we only change when forced to, typically after a big challenge in our life.

This is what happened to me after burnout. I began to value how important I was and could see that it was unsustainable for my health, to keep going in the too-busy, overly-active way I was. I began to recognise how important it was to have me-time to rest and recover from work or friends.

Burnout forced me to get my life together.

### Self-Aware, Hell Yeah!

I had to develop some emotional intelligence and self-awareness around being more mindful of my needs. Developing self-awareness of what I needed in any given moment – whether it be at home racing around the house, doing various chores or looking after our child. Recognising that I needed a break in moments when I was starting to feel worn out was a good start.

If I was out at the shops in amongst the hustle and bustle of noise with people racing around, I would try to be focused on my needs and my goals while I was out – instead of being caught up in the energy and distractions of what other people were doing. So, it was a big step to learn about putting myself first and what my needs were on any given day, in any given moment. It was a hard thing for me to take that step and say no. It actually took a lot of guts.

Courage.

*I rarely stopped or slowed down without suffering first. I mean, only if I was sick, if I had a headache or a cold, would I take a rest. If I was forced to or had no choice. I was always active, busy, ticking off my to-do-list, working hard, moving forward in a never-ending cycle. I was on a treadmill of non-stop, energy-draining activity.*

Looking back now, that was so unsustainable. I couldn't go on that way forever. So, burnout stopped me in the end. For example, even if I was feeling tired, I would go out and do things with friends. I don't know what I was thinking, but I certainly wasn't doing things mindfully or with an awareness of my own needs.

I thought I needed people around me constantly to make me feel good, but that drained my energy too much.

At the time of my burnout, I was doing long hours at work and I was having trouble with my sleeping patterns. But I still tried to maintain my social life, around those long work hours, because I wanted to have a good, fun life. I didn't want to just work – I wanted to live and be around people as much as possible then. However, this outlook meant that I was always pushing myself, instead of putting myself first.

To get your mind onto something else other than what you've been working on is really, really healthy. Do something different, listen to music, be creative, or play a video game – if that's your thing. I just didn't have any emotional intelligence around those things, and I didn't have any guidance either. Ultimately, I didn't look inward to notice what I needed.

I was so used to being on autopilot.

## Mindset: I Am Important

Because I was always doing things to suit other people's needs and not for myself, burnout forced me to really focus on changing my mindset and outlook – about what I truly needed. Once I had forgiven myself for being burnt out and accepted the fact that it wasn't going to be over in a month or two; once I had accepted that I had to be in it for the long haul, then I could move forward. I could actually start to develop a stronger outlook and mindset just for myself, in which I put myself first. It was like a plan for my future.

I put my needs ahead of others and I told myself not to feel bad for doing that.

I don't know where I missed the memo on learning this stuff when I was younger, but basically, I'd grown up in a giving house where we tended to do things for others. We gave time to help people in the community, like the church and the school. We donated things to families in need and sponsored a child, which are generous, community-spirited things to do. It felt good to contribute and was a nice way to be part of the little town where I grew up, which meant we knew lots of people, so it was good in that way. But, although we didn't do it all the time, for me growing up, there was a view, that we should make ourselves available to give, give, give.

I guess that influenced how I approached giving to others later in life, because I didn't know when to stop and when I needed to look at giving to myself, to meet my own needs.

Because of my new mindset and recognising that I am important, too, I told myself that I would try to only say "yes" after considering a few things and checking in with myself first. If I was asked to do something, I would consider these things:

    a) Was it worthwhile?

    b) Would it drain too much of my energy?

    c) What impacts would the activity or task have on me?

It was like retraining my brain to see things in a new light and do things differently.

Because I had never done these checks on myself before, it was really, really hard to remember to consider these things before agreeing. I had developed such an automatic way of instantly saying yes to people.

*I started to break old entrenched habits and teach myself new ways of doing things.*

I changed the way I approached or dealt with people.

At heart, I think I'm quite an introverted and shy person. With the old me, I found it easier to agree to something quickly without having to discuss it further or question the why. Then the conversation could move on or stop after I had agreed. It would be over and I could breathe a big sigh of relief. I could stop feeling uncomfortable as I didn't have to keep talking to the person.

So, a lot of this mindset change was about overcoming a fear of what others thought of me. It took a lot of courage to put myself first. A lot of inner strength to overcome these types of entrenched habits. It felt strange and uncomfortable at first, so I just had to do it over and over again, until it became second nature. Then it wasn't such a struggle to change, or took as much effort to remind myself.

Even today, I still have to work at this. But I truly started getting it together once I started to break away from unhealthy old habits and form healthy new ones.

## Knowing My Needs

It was a scary feeling to bring my new mindset into the world. Although I felt uncertain of who I was, it felt right and was good for me to do. But I was going into the unknown, breaking this image of who others thought I was. This was really challenging. For me, it was one thing to have this mindset and implement it at home with people I was close to, as I could explain myself. But it was another thing to do it in the real world. It was really hard to implement, when I'd always been the kind of person to accept, say yes and agree.

In the face of those old behaviours, trying to convince or put into practice with other people that you're not the same person, was a challenge. I don't behave that way anymore.

I am different now.

A big part of changing my mindset was also changing the mindset of other people that I dealt with regularly. Once I had set myself a goal to do that and change my mindset, I started to say, *"No."*

Often it was my inner self that wanted to say yes, but I really needed to put into practice the art of saying no. So, I started saying no to things, like going out and meeting up with friends if I was feeling tired.

At work, I started questioning tasks that I knew I couldn't manage or complete by a quick deadline. I would try to be more open about what I needed and speak up if my deadlines weren't achievable. I learned to take a break if I needed it. Not to take a break to have coffee with someone, which is what I used to do. But I learnt to put down my mouse, walk away from my computer and just look out the window or have a wander around if I needed to unwind at work.

It's funny, there's a culture in workplaces that you tend to mimic and you don't realise you're doing it.

Think about it. It's really rare to see someone at work, looking out the window, isn't it? I became very conscious of this when it became a regular part of my breaks.

I must say, it takes strength to do that because you're supposed to always be busy at work, right? You're supposed to have your head down and be busy, busy, busy. Reading, analysing, thinking, planning. You're too busy to deal with anything else but the work, the deadline, the end result. No matter what it takes to get there. It's like we're supposed to seem snowed under all the time. Just managing and surviving each day. But I believe that is unsustainable and unhealthy.

There's a culture of this kind of behaviour in some workplaces. I really had to retrain myself amidst that type of culture that it was okay to take a break. It was okay to look out the window for five minutes. I mean, no-one ever specifically questioned what I was doing, but when you're the only one looking out the window, people notice. When it's an open plan office, people notice these sorts of things.

That gave me a sense that I wasn't doing what I 'should' be doing – working.

Because even though they say it's about work-life balance and managing your own workload, who teaches you those things? Unless you learn them growing up or at university, then you don't have a chance to change.

The trouble with me is that when I'm really focused and in the work zone, I find it really hard to pull away from what I'm doing to even take a break. But a ten-minute break is not much time out of an eight-hour day. It's like the old cigarette break, when people used to go outside for a cigarette, they weren't looking at the computer – they were having a break! They probably should have been breathing in fresh air, but they were still having a break.

So, that's how I think of it - having my own cigarette break. I'm not a smoker and never have been, but it's the only analogy I could think of that makes sense.

Then I started to not take extra things on in the lunch hour. Except for a weekly yoga class I did, I would keep most of my lunch hours free during the week. I mean, they were only half an hour, but I used to generally be one of those people who had a full calendar. I used to feel uncomfortable if I didn't have anything on at lunch. If I wasn't catching up with a friend, or doing some exercise during a lunch break, being alone or inactive felt strange to me.

*One of the biggest changes I made was that I purposefully made peace with not committing to anything during my lunch breaks. I would just sit outside on my own and enjoy my lunch, breathing in the fresh outside air while watching the birds darting from tree to tree.*

The other catch was, I would try to not look at my phone while on a break. The phone is always there, pulling at us, wanting us to check something, buy something, post or message someone. So, I would try not to look at my phone. Phones are good fillers. They fill up empty, otherwise quiet spaces with 'white noise', to cover up our uncomfortable feelings, so we don't have to feel like we're really alone.

When we feel like we just need something, but we don't really know what it is, what do we do?

We pick up our phones and scroll through some stuff, read the news or see if we have any messages. Phones were a space filler and an unhealthy distraction that took me away from noticing my feelings and checking in with myself.

So, I changed.

I turned off my notifications and put my phone on mute, so nothing would alert me to check it. Let's face it, notifications from social media aren't that pressing and can usually wait. If it was really important, someone would call or message me and I would hear it vibrating.

Eventually, I started to enjoy precious me time, being on my own at lunch. I would sit outside or take a stroll around the building, look up at the sky and watch the clouds moving by. And every so often, I would meet a friend to catch up. But I certainly didn't fill up my days anymore.

Because of burnout, I couldn't.

It's hard to change unless we are forced to.

Unless we face a major life or health challenge, we tend to sit with what we know; the status quo. But I am glad that burnout made me change the unhealthy habits I had. The way I didn't notice what I needed and let others convince me that they knew what was best. Maybe it was the wakeup call I needed to change.

Although I wish I had the energy I used to readily burn, burnout reminds me to this day, to tune into my needs.

*Once I had accepted that burnout floored me for a reason, then I could make my own positive changes. I could reassess my needs and redefine what I truly needed, in order to move forward on a new, calmer path.*

That was a good thing.

The pace of today's world and the pressures that we have to contend with, place so many demands on us. The pressures don't ask us if we mind shouldering them, they just exist without question. So, if we let all those pressures; the expectations of others, family commitments and the 24/7 pull of technology, demand too much of us, it can make us unwell. Therefore, we need to be more self-aware and notice what effect those pressures are having and how they stress us out. Then we can take action.

Because if we let the pressures and stress get the better of us, then we won't be able to function at all.

Burnout is not a pleasant thing to happen, believe me. It derails the sense of who you are and made me feel so utterly exhausted mentally and physically, that I had no more to give to anyone, including myself.

That is not a way to live.

We need to be wiser to the demands of the modern world. Stand up against it, rather than submit to it. Otherwise, it will chew you up and spit you out. It won't say thanks for all your sacrifices and hard work. No, you will more than likely be left on your own to deal with the negative and unexpectedly, long-lasting fallout.

## Chapter Eight

# Healing Together

*"At times our own light goes out and is rekindled by a spark from another person. Each of us has cause to think with deep gratitude of those who have lighted the flame within us."*

(Albert Schweitzer)

For me, having burnout and getting through it was a time of isolation. I spent lots of time alone to rest and recover. But, I also felt alone in what I was going through. I discovered that too much solitary time is unhealthy and can torment the mind.

It's a struggle being alone, feeling like you're the only person in the world going through this challenge.

But you are not alone, believe me.

I now know others who have experienced burnout themselves. It's so much more common than you think. Especially in today's world, where we have so many commitments and others' needs to satisfy, as well as our seemingly endless to-do lists.

So, how did I get through it? Well, finding and establishing a reliable support network was a big part of my recovery. This network included close friends and family, and medical and wellness professionals. Together, these people helped me to heal and recover from burnout.

## Wellbeing Keys Unlocked

The key was finding people to talk to, people who I trusted and who cared for me. I told really close friends about what happened, about the struggle I faced with burnout. Knowing people who I felt safe with were so important when I was feeling vulnerable.

It helped me to feel less isolated and less alone.

Friends that were there for me and supported me no matter what. If you have that, then I believe you'll get through your burnout a lot quicker. Although the downside of suffering burnout for me was, I found some people who I thought were friends, weren't true friends. They were people that I thought would be there to help me, but they weren't.

It's unfortunate and I was saddened by it at the time because it was yet another thing to deal with. But it can happen.

I don't know why; I can only assume that some people felt uncomfortable about always having to counsel or support my needs. I understand that certain people might want to be in that position. I chose to let go of a friend or two, so I could move forward.

Instead, I focused on friends who were there for me in the bad, as well as the good times.

My wellbeing support network was also professionals. I found a counsellor to start off with after I first burnt out. I accessed the service provided by my employer, who I saw as often as I could – I think I went every two weeks. But I was seeing different counsellors each visit and found that a bit inconsistent as I had to re-tell my story each time. I later found a psychologist, who I still rely on today when the need arises.

I also saw my General Practitioner (GP) and a naturopath for different reasons. The GP I was seeing at the time, didn't recognise my burnout symptoms. I was prescribed sleeping tablets to try to establish a better sleep pattern. But it was disappointing that burnout was beyond their scope of understanding and I later discovered that it's not recognised by traditional doctors.

Then I saw a naturopath and everything changed (e.g. Appendix A).

She recognised burnout and I received an assessment and health plan going forward. I enjoyed going to see her as I felt really looked after and had a positive strategy to assist my energy levels and tiredness. She recognised that I was dealing with adrenal fatigue, which was heartening.

Practitioners of complementary medicine assisted me after I was failed by others. I could call these people any time and make an appointment, so I knew I wasn't alone.

*I didn't have all the answers – I'd never experienced anything like burnout before – I realised I had to ask for help if I was going to improve. So, I sought their help, guidance and support, and in the end, I found the right people for me.*

I can't emphasize enough how important it was to feel safe and supported.

It got me through tough times, when my mood got low and I felt as if I would have burnout forever. If you just can't think of anyone and you're feeling really alone and low, then there's always help online or just a phone call away.

We are extremely lucky these days to be able to access a range of supports to help find the key to our wellness (e.g. Appendix A; *Beyond Blue, Perinatal Wellbeing Centre*).

When I felt I needed expert advice, I put aside my self-doubt and limiting beliefs, picked up the phone and called some of these organisations. Keep in mind that they may not be the perfect person to talk to. I found out that a counsellor doesn't have to be perfect, because the chat broke a cycle of repetitive thinking I was going through. I also had the option of hanging up and calling another organisation if I wanted to.

My sense of wellbeing was all over the place. I felt uncertain, lacked confidence and couldn't see a clear way forward. At times I sat alone in my room, crying about the failure I felt, the shame of it all and grieving all that I had lost. I just cried and released all that emotion, but I felt alone in those feelings.

I couldn't keep talking to my partner about some of these things. Couldn't bring it up again and again as I felt it was coming between us. I decided I needed to talk to someone more neutral and removed from my situation.

In a moment of crisis, I picked up the phone and spoke to a counsellor. Not every time I was struggling, because there were times I just wanted to hide away from the world and be with my feelings. But I was glad the times I did call. I found it was good to talk to someone on a phone call and not face to face, because I felt safe being at home. I had my comfy slippers on and sat in my comfy chair with a cup of tea and had a bit of a teary chat.

*I found that another person's perspective, helped me start to see things more clearly. So that I could see a way forward and might not feel so drained by burnout, forever.*

## Calming Connections

Another thing I found really important was to connect with others. It was so important for me to get out of my head, to stop thinking so much and dwelling on what I was going through and think about other things.

There were (and are) other things going on in the world.

It wasn't all about burnout and the struggles I was going through. So, I took up flute lessons – I had always wanted to learn and I thought music would be a good way for my brain to repair itself. I bought a second-hand flute and found a local lady to do weekly lessons with. It was motivating to have a hobby to look forward to each week that challenged me a little bit and took me out of my comfort zone.

It was one-on-one so I didn't have to be in a big group of people and it was something creative that took my mind to a different place, away from work and my troubles. Sometimes I didn't feel like going every week, but I kept it up anyway, even if I was worn out or tired. Sometimes I felt really tired after work, but it was a nice distraction from my issues. There are so many things on offer these days, such as knitting at your local café, a bushwalking group, a book club or attending church – try to find something that you like the sound of.

I really tried to keep attending things in person and tried not to retreat away from the world too much. Spending too much time on my phone wasn't healthy and I believe interacting with people in person has many more benefits for the soul and life outlook anyway.

*One of my favourite things to do is to get out in nature.*

It's somewhere I feel safe, a place that I can really relax. I love to take a walk and sit on a big rock down next to the river, listening to the stream bubbling past, or watching the water moving and leaves floating down. It's just so soothing to do this sort of thing.

Although I used to go to the gym a few days a week before I burnt out, I didn't go back straight away. I used to go for walks around the neighbourhood in the fresh air instead. Breathing fresh air and getting my blood pumping around my body was so beneficial. Plus, I enjoyed watching the antics of the magpies, galahs and currawongs in my area.

At this time, I kept my exercise to lower impact things and didn't do any high intensity classes with loud music. Eventually I started to do workouts on my own at the gym on the cross trainer – with my earplugs in!

I found exercise was a really important way to get through burnout because it changes the brain chemicals from negative to positive ones. I found that working out at too high intensity, which really got my heart rate up, generated feelings of anxiety, especially in the early stages of burnout. But it was such a good feeling to get the blood pumping around my body again. So much so, that I had to reign myself in and not exercise for too long, otherwise the benefits would be outweighed by feelings of being totally sapped of energy.

My recovery was a real balancing act.

Early on in burnout, I didn't see friends or family too much, I just wanted to be alone so I could learn how to be calm again. So, I replenished my social needs by going to the shops or sitting at a café. I was surrounded by people doing normal things, which I found very, very healing. I didn't have to tell them the whole story of my burnout or explain what I was going through. It was nice and easy. Sometimes I could lose myself in just observing others.

Generally we're social creatures and enjoy the company of others, for the feel-good vibes they radiate.

This is something that worked for me, and helped me heal. I avoided noisy cafes and found a quiet one where I could be near people. I also used to go to the park on my own and just sit in the sun and watch kids play in the playground or watch people exercising, going about their business. It was nice to see other people doing positive things. I recommend finding somewhere you like to spend non-interactive time to be around people.

It was very healing for me.

## Your Burnout Stories

Through my burnout journey, I discovered other people who had also experienced burnout. Without doubt, there would be people at your workplace or someone you know who has experienced a form of burnout during their life. After my experience at work, other people quietly came and told me about their experience of burnout. A senior manager revealed that he experienced burnout when he had young kids many years ago.

He was a professional high-achiever who was always on the go.

He travelled a lot for work and always had lots of meetings to prepare for. I could see how that could happen. Another colleague at work, said an old friend had experienced burnout. He couldn't manage the relentless, high output of work that was expected. So it started to take a toll.

The unrealistic and high expectations of senior staff and pressure to succeed in certain industries, is really high. Not everyone is cut out for that.

*Some people can handle more pressure and a higher workload than others. But continued, intense periods of hard work or working long hours to achieve a major body of work, can take a toll on us.*

It's not for everyone, which I found out. I couldn't keep up the pace that other people seem to work at. I couldn't keep up the reading, the research, the analysis, the meetings. In the end, it just took too much out of me and depleted my energy. Until I started to run on empty.

Another colleague told me she experienced burnout as a mining geologist. She found that because she was a woman working in a male-dominated industry, she always had to work twice as hard to prove she was half as good as her male colleagues. Although she was an experienced geologist, she was often given menial tasks to complete and her geological expertise were questioned (although she had a bona fide science degree), which was demeaning and put a lot of unnecessary stress on her.

Then she discovered that she was getting paid half of what a male colleague was receiving in an equivalent role. So, she asked her boss about increasing her pay rate, which created more workplace stress. Then, after working long hours on a demanding shift work roster to do the required duties, taking on additional tasks to prove herself over and over again, along with dealing with demeaning and dismissive comments, her job ended in burnout.

Overall, she found that being treated as a graduate employee every time she worked at a new mine site, and having to continually prove her ability as a scientist, was exhausting. It took a toll on her self-esteem and she started to feel disconnected and lack the energy required to complete her work. She said that slowly, she felt her initial passion for the field of STEMM fade away. She wasn't receiving the positive outcomes she wanted, for the personal investment she was making in her career.

It is unfortunate that women are still treated with such little professional respect in male-dominated industries such as mining. The pressure that arose from her ill-treatment, led to stress and burnout. After all her hard work and 12 years in the industry, burnout forced her to leave for good. After a six-month sabbatical to recover, she resumed work, but never returned to mining.

Another story I was told about, involved a mama who had three young children, who managed the bulk of the family work and children at home as her husband often worked away. She got burnout trying to manage the household, the daily needs of the children, the house work, the drop offs and the multitude of things that is expected of a mama. She was trying to be superwoman, pushing herself to the limit with minimal help from others. Until it all got too much for her and she realised she was running on empty without enough time to recover and recuperate. After months of this, eventually she couldn't keep up with the constant demands of her family.

Its relentless, the many, small, thankless tasks that are required of a mama, and if you're not managing everything well, getting the help you need or maintaining your balance, it can lead to burnout.

My own mum experienced burnout. It was caused from a head injury after she got hit in the head with the boom of a boat. At first, she didn't realise there was anything wrong, but a CT scan revealed a fractured skull. She had to give up working as a teacher of young children, finding she couldn't be as busy as she was, or maintain her other commitments. Burnout affected her sleep, concentration and appetite. She got headaches and during her recovery had to rest and just listened to music all day.

If she went for a walk or was exposed to intense stimulation – like shopping centres – she would start to feel dizzy, so she had to limit her activity. After six months of that she gradually returned to work, but she thinks it took about four years for most of her symptoms to disappear. Much longer to regain her fitness and feel 'normal' again.

Burnout really can happen in different ways.

*It has been a real comfort to me as I progressed through my own journey of burnout to know that other people have also experienced it.*

To me, it means that we're all fallible in a demanding world, not failures. It's just that some of us can break if we're pushed to our limits. Is anyone really resilient enough to get through all the commitments and pressures we have in today's world without feeling the stress of it?

It's a real challenge.

**Overwork is Real**

Contending with overwork is real for many. People who regularly work long hours – such as those in senior management roles and those who work 24/7 rosters or do overtime – frequently push themselves to their limits. This kind of work isn't without a cost to personal health, with impacts on sleeping patterns, hormone levels and heart problems. For example, people who do shift work have an increased risk of health problems, such as heart disease, obesity and accidents, due to daytime sleepiness. (State Government of Victoria, 2020)

These include people like journalists, medical professionals, paramedics, miners, surveillance, security and factory workers, and police, nurses and firemen.

These people are likely to develop unhealthy habits because of the nature of their work. They are used to pushing themselves through working long hours, in intense and stressful scenarios while tired. They may be in a damaging cycle of running on autopilot, continually pushing themselves. When exhaustion is a regular thing, I believe it exposes them to the risk of burnout.

This is what I was doing when burnout floored me - contributing to work beyond my normal capacity. I was on a shift roster and asked to do overtime if there was a shortage of staff. I was up at night when I should have been asleep, disrupting my circadian rhythms and melatonin. Plus, I was in a state of chronic sleep deprivation when I suffered burnout.

*I was not mindful of the over work that I was participating in because my judgement was masked by an overwhelming tiredness.*

I believe that working long hours and ensuing sleep deprivation, also has impacts on emotional wellbeing. Potentially exposing us to mental health problems like anxiety. Just like I experienced.

This is real.

So, I am concerned for these people. As it may not be something they notice straight away – burnout can creep up when we believe we have adjusted to pushing ourselves. But then we become exhausted and wham!

All of a sudden you aren't capable of managing all the demands as you used to. Your energy levels are depleted. Everything becomes more challenging than it used to be. Things like maintaining your workload and normal day-to-day tasks become harder, then throw in something extra like taking care of a sick family member and suddenly you're on the road to burnout. Believe me – I have experienced it myself.

If we want to avoid a society of workers with burnout, we need to recognise the potential impact the work we do, could have on our future health.

Some days it feels like walking on a tightrope as we juggle more balls than should be possible. Maybe we are juggling too much. We need to check in and ensure that we haven't taken on more than is possible and if we are working at a healthy limit for ourselves.

I hope this provides others with some comforting insights that they're not alone in what they're going through. It may even be a wake-up call as to how common it potentially is among our colleagues, friends and family.

## Chapter Nine

# My Recovery Secrets

*"There are days I drop words of comfort on myself like falling leaves and remember that it is enough to be taken care of by myself."*

(Brian Andrews)

As a result of my burnout experience, I found several secrets that really supported my recovery. The key was really about being kind to myself. Once I learnt how to be truly kind to myself, developed new positive habits and implemented a self-care routine, I could make real progress towards recovery.

Firstly, I did some research online to find out about what other people had done to manage their burnout and I could only find snippets of information here and there. At that time, there didn't seem to be a lot of information focused solely on burnout and its recovery. There was a lot around managing stress and overwork though, which proved useful. I found information on meditation and mindfulness techniques, and yoga and relaxation. Some strategies worked really well for me and were easy and accessible to implement, which led me to develop these practical burnout hacks and secrets for recovery.

## Time Alone to Just Be

Along my path to recovery, I battled internally to manage my needs for quiet and healing, along with my need to be as normal as possible – which weren't compatible at all.

I really needed that alone time during my recovery. I just needed peace and quiet to relax. And I needed to rest my brain. I didn't want to listen to, or deal with challenging people or tasks. I just wanted to limit my stress levels and the social anxiety that had resulted from burnout.

It's what I needed, but it was a double-edged sword because the more time I spent alone, I realised I actually needed to be with people. I needed to start managing that, so I didn't feel so sad and alone.

It was an ongoing battle to manage my needs.

I flipped between, working and then not working, being alone and not wanting to be alone. It was really challenging to get the right balance.

## My Recovery Secrets

Now, I realise the value of alone time.

I also needed to pause and to value the pause, rather than finding it was slowing me down. I used to switch so quickly between tasks at work – or send a message on the phone then quickly do a task at home – that I forgot to pause. But I really needed to pause between activities more after burnout. I needed to be more conscious and aware of changing between activities, which really gave me space to breathe and reconnect with myself.

These things have been so valuable during my recovery – although I sometimes I forget and find myself falling back into old habits. But I can recognize I'm doing it now before it gets out of hand, pull myself up and pause, breathe and start over again.

Having alone time to recharge today as a mama is also really important to me. It can be really hard as a mama to get alone time. When the days are so full and busy with looking after a child, being alone can help me feel calm, safe and in touch with my needs.

I have found ways to etch out little moments during the day to just be alone. For me, that means looking out the window at the lovely blue sky or the clouds rushing past or just gazing out into the green space outside my window. When I go to the bathroom (which is often one of the only times you get alone as a mama with a young child) or when I'm making a cup of tea, I take three deep breaths and just focus on the kettle boiling and making the tea. I use that time to check in with myself, do some breathing and to see how I'm tracking.

*Having time to be and be alone is so rare these days when our lives are so full to the brim. Making time to be quiet and still while surrounded by busyness can be hard.*

To just be in the world and breathe. It's about gratitude really, realizing that its ok to just soak up the sun or the view or the peaceful surrounds of your favourite place, wherever that might be. Just to realise how lucky you are to have that space.

I found it challenging at first, just to let go of all the things I was thinking about, planning, and doing. So many things pass through our minds if we let them. But once I valued stillness more, I could let those things go. So, I would sit outside in a quiet place, like beneath a big elm tree I have at the front of my house and enjoy the day. Remove myself from the hectic pace of my surroundings and enjoy being there in my green space.

Letting it wash over me. Letting the breeze flow through me. Letting the sounds of the leaves and birds above, filter in. So, I wasn't thinking of anything else, for a minute or two. Then, for the briefest of moments, I can escape my busy mind and sense inner peace.

## Solving Burnout at Work

When it came to managing burnout at work, the biggest factor was to reduce my work hours. Straight after the burnout, I had about six weeks off work, and then gradually returned to work, where I did four to five hours a day. I started off by doing 9am-1pm, five days a week.

As I improved, I built up from there, going 9am-2pm and I think I stayed at 9am- 3pm for quite a while. I had support from my workplace health officer and had a really supportive manager who didn't put any extra pressure on me – or have big expectations of me. It was a new job as I'd left my job that had led to burnout.

Starting this new job, even though I was not functioning at my full capacity, I was so thankful that he took me on. He gave me small achievable tasks that were really attainable. Having that support was so helpful in believing in myself again and feeling comfortable at work. Feeling normal at work really aided my recovery and positive mindset for the future.

At an office job, I was on the computer most of the time. One of my biggest challenges was that switching between tasks made me feel anxious. For example, I used to switch between my email and a spreadsheet or another document I was working on and a spreadsheet, checking data. Instead of quickly flicking between each, like I used to, I tried to really slow this down and make it more purposeful, so it was easier for my brain to adapt. Plus, I had to get away from the computer screen roughly every 30 to 40 minutes.

I used to get this brain fog, where all the information just seemed to be very slow to register, which I took to be a sign of overwhelm.

So, I'd just walk to the toilet, look out the window or have a walk around my office area and come back. After burnout, I just couldn't sit there for the duration of time that I used to.

Focusing on slowing my breathing down was a big part of keeping my anxiety at bay, as well as slowing down my reactivity and the fight or flight response I often felt.

It was hard being at work, surrounded by all the activity and background noise. It would have been great if working from home was as accepted then as it is now, due to the pandemic.

Back then, I had to jump through so many hoops to make it happen, get a desk assessment at home, safety assessment, set up my internet. It all seemed too much for me being on my own at the time, to set all this up when I couldn't think clearly and make good decisions.

So, I ended up working in the office among all the busyness, where it was a constant battle to maintain a sense of calm. I couldn't lie down there either, which made it hard - sometimes I just felt like lying down for a ten-minute rest. There was nowhere I could do that really at work that was acceptable – except when I was doing yoga.

## My Five Recovery Secrets

### 1. Yoga and Breathing

Yoga is something that I found really useful for calming and grounding myself and getting out of my head and into my body. I'd already done yoga for years, having first started while I was at university. But it became even more important in my recovery from burnout. I already attended a weekly class with other people. (e.g. Appendix A, Antidote Yoga, Kendra Healing Arts)

This tapered off a little bit after initial burnout because I ended up being at home a fair bit. But I had access to yoga books and already knew my favourite postures and breathing practices, so I would do some stretches at home. I usually like to do cat-cow, bridge and the spinal twist for core release and gentle movement – and do mountain pose, pigeon and child's pose for calmness and grounding.

If it was a sunny day, I'd go out in the sun, absorbing that lovely vitamin D and do yoga stretches outside. It would help me to replenish that lost energy, focus on the movement of my body and feel calm, immersed in my green space with Wattlebirds and Noisy Miner birds darting overhead.

I can also access yoga anywhere on my phone. When I need a bit more guidance and inspiration, I like to use the *Down Dog* and *Yoga Go* apps. These are good for giving me a more structured and timed routine for different parts of the body. I really like the *'Unwind Your Body'* and *'De-Stressing Yoga'* workouts.

*Yoga was also really helpful to calm my breathing. When I was wound up and feeling anxious, my breathing and heart rate would be quite rapid. So, I needed to slow down my breathing, stop that fight or flight response and get calm.*

The best breathing to help calm the nervous system is one where you have a slower exhale than inhale. Breathe in to a count of four, then exhale to a count of six and then extend the exhalation more with practice. Doing three of these breath cycles is a quick way to calm stress or anxiety levels.

Regular yoga was really helpful to help develop resilience and calm breathing techniques that I could call upon when needed.

Once I had these tools, I could implement them when I was feeling stressed or anxious. To concentrate on breathing as a way of winding down and escaping stress was extremely beneficial for burnout recovery and also a way to practice being kind to myself. I still rely on these techniques today.

### 2. Nature and Exercise

Simplicity was a big part of my recovery. Enjoying simple, easy things that didn't put any pressure on me like being outside in nature. I felt comfortable surrounded by nature and it was a really important way for me to relax. I would go for long walks in the reserve near where I lived and focus on my breathing. Sometimes I would do a walking meditation, where you focus on putting one foot in front of the other in sync with your breath e.g. inhale, right foot forward; exhale, left foot forward. I'd do that and just walk along the path on my own and watched kangaroos and their joeys or listened to the birds up in the trees, twittering and darting around. I just really valued getting out for long walks and hated it when it was cold or wintry or raining outside.

When it was windy, it didn't really prevent me from going anywhere. I just rugged up with my beanie and jacket. But if it was raining, I'd feel a bit more trapped at home with an over-active mind. Escaping outside helped to ease excessive thinking and internalising my thoughts.

Looking out at the horizon is also something that I found helped centre myself. So, I'd walk up where I could get a nice view out to the hills and get away from everything; my problems, my burnout. The value of getting your heart rate up, with exercise and then learning to wind down from that exercise afterwards was also helpful to develop resilience and calm myself after exertion.

### 3. Meditation

Meditation was – and still is – a wonderful relaxation technique that helped my body and mind find peace and stillness after all it had been through. I now have a meditation practice and integrate it most days. Before burning out, I had dabbled in meditation here and there, but I'd never truly needed it. But after burnout, meditation was something that I had to try and incorporate into my life on a daily basis. Although it helped me to wind down, I resisted doing it at first and just didn't feel like I should have to change my routine. I wasn't comfortable with the way burnout had forced me to make these changes and meditate (stubborn I know!).

I found a phone app with mindfulness meditations I liked, called *Calm*. I found it really accessible as a person who was just learning the ropes. It provides short guided mindfulness meditations and has a lot of different features, including tracking your progress, relaxing music and quotes of the day, which I liked.

Initially I used the free version, but I discovered many more features once I subscribed. It was money worth spending, money used to help my recovery. I have tried so many of these meditations now. Some that truly assisted my recovery were: *'Seven Days of Calming Anxiety", "Breaking Habits Series", "Emotions Series", "Seven Days of Managing Stress"* and *"Relaxation for Sleep."*

The *'Body Scan'* was really useful for relaxing my muscles from my head to my toes, to get rid of tension at the end of a busy day and is something I still use. I also did *'Daily Calm'* which is a quick, 10-minute meditation that has a different topic every day. There are so many meditation options and early in my recovery, I didn't know of many useful tools for burnout, but the meditation app was often my one point of call that I could just rely on instantly to help slow myself down.

### 4. Creativity and Mindfulness

I had ignored my creative side for too long and needed to incorporate it into my life again as a path to finding calm. I discovered art therapy through mindful colouring-in, which was wonderful and easy. I already had a few colouring-in books that I'd hardly used – along with my Derwent colour pencils from school. So, I dug them out after many years collecting dust and made it part of my day as a way to de-stress. I often did colouring-in after work, when I was feeling really stressed.

I found that if I focused on just colouring and did it slowly without setting any goals, then I could just focus on colouring and let the creative part of my brain take over. Having such an analytical job, it was wonderful to be colouring in some nice flowers with a selection of colours that I'd chosen, something completely different from work. It was so soothing and relaxing for me.

*Taking time to incorporate mindful practices into the things I did, helped me to slow down and pause in between activities. I'd always been a go, go, go type of person, and mindfulness helped me understand the value of slowing down and so I integrated it into everyday moments.*

Mindfulness helped me to focus on one thing when I was accustomed to thinking about multiple things at once. For example, I tried to use moments like brushing my teeth, to solely focus on looking in the mirror and brushing, slowly and mindfully. I needed to retrain my brain to stop over-thinking and used everyday moments to put mindfulness into action.

Eating is another thing where I would usually be looking at my phone, chatting or reading at the same time. I often forgot to enjoy the food and the act of eating. So, I would slow down and purposefully chew each mouthful and notice the taste of the food. It was hard to change, but the end result was I savoured my meals (and I didn't get the hiccups as much anymore!).

### 5. Quiet Relaxation

Whether it be getting a restful night's sleep or finding ways to be still during the day, quiet relaxation was something I strived for constantly. I couldn't listen to the loud rock music I used to anymore – it didn't help me wind down. Instead, I found soothing nature music, ambient relaxation, soothing classical and tranquil world playlists on *Spotify* or *Calm*. I got into the habit of playing relaxing music if I was feeling a bit stressed or wound up. I listened to music at night to help me wind down or during my lunch breaks at work to escape from stress.

In order to relax, I also needed to manage the time spent looking at my phone. The way I started to do this was to turn off my notifications (especially the social media ones) and put my phone on mute. I needed to do this to reduce my hyper-alert state and stop checking it so regularly. It's so hard to switch off to our phones, but I think it can be an added stressor when it alerts us 24/7 and is a source of all types of information, tasks and reminders.

This is especially the case when we are trying to overcome something like burnout.

I have never been someone who left the phone on next to me when I slept. Following a meditation or listening to relaxing music, I'd always turned it off at night. I don't know how we can really rest when we have such a powerful tool left turned on, right next to us, constantly alerting and distracting us.

I would also go for massages a bit more regularly during my recovery, probably once every couple of weeks. It was so lovely to be helped to relax, with the masseur's hands soothing the tension from my body. It helped me when I wasn't sleeping well, felt wound up and stressed. It helped me to get out of my head and into my body. Such bliss! The place that I went to had lovely Thai music playing in the background.

It was just the type of medication I needed at the time.

I still enjoy a massage, of course – who doesn't?! But there were times when I needed to release tension quickly, so I would use self-massage. I hold a lot of stress and tightness in my head, particularly over my forehead and eye brows.

So, I would find a quiet spot to sit and close my eyes and use both hands to gently rub in small circles. But I also discovered a place above my ears near the temples, where I can release a lot of the tightness in my whole head, if I massage there. It's not noticeably tight, but when I rub it gently, I find I can release a lot of tension across my entire head, from my eye brows, jaw and face.

*Learning to be kind to myself through these self-care techniques was the key to my recovery. Once I had found the things that worked for me, I could call on them when needed. The biggest positive change was carving out quiet time in my day, to be alone and still. It was habit-forming.*

It was also a new thing to be kind to myself at work. I had to train myself how I wanted to act and be at work. This wasn't easy as co-workers had a certain impression of me. But because I started to value alone time more, I would implement that at work as well. Giving myself space and not putting pressure on myself to 'be' anything other than what I needed. So, I learnt to be more authentic at work and to tune into my needs.

I started to care less about what others thought of me and wasn't the yes person I'd always been, any longer.

## My Recovery Secrets

These secrets are accessible to anyone who wishes to implement self-care habits in their day. Whether its stress from work, feeling over worked, or general busyness from too many commitments, these recovery secrets are the sure-fire chillout hacks we all need to survive in a busy world. It's not just about giving to others, if we want to get through each day and feel well at days end, we need to give back to ourselves.

Give yourself some comfort, kindness and gentleness, and sooth away the ever-present stress in your life.

## Chapter Ten

# Living Not Giving

*"Through loving kindness, everyone and everything can flower again from within."*

(Sharon Salzberg)

Despite going through several challenges; leaving a long-term partner, the pressures of being a new mama, the demands working from home with a young child and the COVID cauldron during 2020, these were all overshadowed by my burnout experience. Due to that, thankfully, I now know so many more things about myself.

I know I can't be the giver I once was.

I can't give away my time, my energy, and ultimately my inner peace so easily anymore. I now realise how important it is to treasure those things, to look after them and keep them safe. I can no longer give all those things away so easily without first considering the impacts it might have on me and my family.

I can live the life I want, without life impacting on me as much as it used to, if I put those things first. It was a long, winding road to get to this place, with some unexpected hurdles along the way, but I believe I have now arrived in a calmer, more peaceful place to live.

## Present Emma 2.0

Emma 2.0 lives in the present, constantly learning. I don't think I'll ever give up learning about myself and how to improve my way of being in this demanding world. I now know I'm vulnerable to its pressures and expectations, so I have more self-awareness around it. I see it as a constantly evolving thing, still learning how to be the new, calmer me.

With everything I know now, I can recognise the warning signs that I might be overdoing it or giving too much of my energy away. I now understand that the twitching sensations I feel in my face, my heavy head or my short temper and snappy responses, indicate that it's time to take a break. It's time to take a few breaths and somehow find calm.

Now I know I need to limit the time I spend in crowds, in shops and in noisy groups of people. I'm more at ease in knowing that. But also knowing within myself that I can spend a short amount of time in these places. If I spend too long, I know how it will impact me.

I know that interacting with people that talk too much or talk too loudly, drains my energy. I know that I can talk to these people, but that I can also get away when I want to. I am stronger now and know that I can remove myself from draining or busy situations if I need to.

I can get away, if I need to. I can simply walk away.

I now know that the warning signs and sensations I feel are the start of me feeling stressed. If I deal with the stress, the sensations will gradually fade away. If I don't, they will worsen and might lead to stronger feelings of anxiety and take longer to subside. But I also know that they will subside and fade eventually. I don't have to get into a cycle of anxiety or feel scared that I will feel that way forever. My emotions and the sensasions I feel, will all change and dissipate eventually.

Nothing stays the same forever.

*The new me says no a lot more to things. Things that take my energy and that I know will drain and deplete me.*

The old job I had was a major energy-depleting factor and was a huge reason for my initial burnout. The pressure it put on me, the way it made me so tired, created anxious feelings, tension and ultimately made me scared to be there. Now I know I never have to be that person again and never have to feel pressure like that again – because I can say no to things like that. I can say no to things that are damaging for me, that impact on my health or that stress me out too much.

Because those things aren't good for me and my sense of wellbeing.

Of course, it's so hard to say no, to down tools and take a rest when you're doing something you love. I find it really hard to stop writing because I feel great when I am making progress and doing good work. But I know there is no point pushing myself to just complete the paragraph I'm working on. If I feel like a break, I remind myself again and again, to stop and give myself time to just breathe (something that was hard to do while writing this book!).

I'm not perfect by any means.

I am not saying that I'm completely cured. However, I'm more self-aware, more grounded and have better self-judgement now. I know who I am and what I need. I know where to seek help if I need it, because I couldn't overcome a big thing like burnout on my own. We need experts in our corner to help give us the tools we need to get over hurdles and struggles that come up.

## Living Not Giving

We need to keep our loved ones close.

We need friends and family to support us not only when we are doing well, but also when we are struggling. I have found my people. I'm more settled in myself than I've ever been.

I now value the pause.

I'm more content to breathe and just be in the moment. Whether it be while I'm working and need to take a break or whether it's buzzing around doing chores at home, I will pause and take a rest to breathe. At home, I know those chores will always be there. If I get one done quicker, it doesn't mean the other one will also get done quicker. I know that if I speed clean the bathroom, that I will have less energy to do the vacuuming. The amount of energy spent on one activity, will have a flow-on affect into the next one. So, I pause more now.

The new me knows there are hormones at play with how much energy I'm feeling.

I know that in the earlier part of my cycle I am more active, plan more and make progress towards my goals. In this part of my cycle, I need to be careful I don't overdo it as I can easily transition into stress and overwhelm. During the second part of my cycle, I need to slow down and give myself more time to be grounded and calm and not expect as much of myself. The transition between the two parts of my cycle is key for me. Because if I don't recognise it happening and don't give myself a chance to recharge at this time, then I will become stressed, anxious and upset.

It's a balance with my hormones, but I am at peace with these changes now and I am becoming more aware each time.

## Love Thy Self

A big change that has happened during my burnout journey, is that I now give myself more love and kindness. I see how important it is to love yourself first, because without that, you can't give yourself what you need.

I now recognise the value of self-care.

The value of walks outside, being in nature, listening to the birds and breathing the fresh air. The value of having regular breaks away from the computer screen, the phone and the ever-present information overload. I believe that our modern brains can't accommodate so much information from so many sources, without repercussions on our health. I love myself enough to be balanced and not solely focus on work anymore. I know this can come at huge personal cost and now, I love myself too much to let that happen again.

As a mama, I value me-time so highly.

That precious time is so hard to get, so now I value it all the more. I value having a massage when I can. With a young child, I etch out some me-time each day so I can feel balanced and at peace within myself.

During the day, I focus on my body and breathing more, I look out the window when I make a cup of tea or take three deep breaths when I'm in the bathroom. I value these small moments, because they have a calming effect on my body and at the end of the day, I won't feel so worn out.

I value the importance of a daily meditation practice.

Sometimes it's 10 minutes and sometimes its 20 minutes, but I will always open my meditation app and do a meditation or two at the end of the day. Meditation helps me wind down, refocus and reset my busy mind from what's happened during the day. I value being grounded and feeling grounded, whether that means sitting on the floor or lying outside on the grass. Being grounded for me is an important way of helping me find calm – taking my shoes off and walking around barefoot is such a lovely thing to do for your spirit.

I know that I'm important now.

I have learned to stick up for myself and stick up for my needs above all else, apart from my family, of course. I no longer put myself second. Well, as mamas we tend to put ourselves second, but I put myself second less than I used to. I'm more aware and I know I've got this. It's tough being a mama at times, we go through rough times as our children go through their phases – whether its teething, developmental leaps or learning to deal with their own emotions.

As parents, we just have to accept these changes. Together, we've been through a few of these now and at times, I just wanted to curl up in the corner and wish it all away. It was hard for me at first as a burnout mama. But now I know I can get through tough times and don't doubt myself as much. Now I know I can face these tough times, even though its hard and even if I'm tired. In a calm and considered way, I can now manage everything I need to at home to make it work. There have been times in the past where I doubted my ability in every corner of my life. But now, by loving myself, I know that I can get through the challenges that life throws at me.

*I know that with a slower pace and by giving myself more time to think and breathe, I will get there in the end.*

## Chill Out Mindset

Ultimately, I have a new outlook on how I approach my life and a mindset that helps me determine how much energy I give away. Let's start by saying a little mantra I learnt. This is something that serves me well and I can draw on when I need it: *"I am loving, I am kind, but my energy is mine."*

I find it's helpful sometimes to look outward away from what you're going through in order to give yourself a different perspective. I feel this mantra helps me look inward at myself, it knows what I'm capable of and helps me to stay strong and value my needs.

## Living Not Giving

I have five words that remind me of things that I need to keep in my life that help me to chill out. I can remember these things because they are written on a post-it note in my phone cover:

1. Creativity
2. Play
3. Meditation
4. Rest
5. Exercise

I find that if I have these things in my life or can work out a way to get these things into my life every day, then I am a calmer, happier person.

Creativity and play are fairly easy with a toddler because we love playing outside together with trucks or a ball or gardening. We love doing craft together, so I get the crayons or pencils out and enjoy drawing lovely patterns on the paper, with scribbles and laughter happening around me. My son and I also like to dance together, which is a great stress-reliever for me, so I put on my favourite tunes and we wriggle and jiggle around the lounge room.

Meditation is something I can do at night time on my own and it's easy because it's a habit now and its easily accessed on my phone.

Sleep is achievable if I'm well rested during the day, haven't overdone it and given there's no hormonal ups and downs, then I can relax and unwind to get good night's sleep now. But if I'm anxious or stressed about something in my life, I meditate. I also use a self-compassion mantra, to be kind to myself when I'm worn out at the end of the day:

*"May I be happy,*

*May I be safe,*

*May I be healthy,*

*May I be at peace."*

Exercise is more of a challenge, though. Even though I am running around after a little person most days, it's not consistent exercise and I'm not exercising the different muscle groups in my body. But I do little things like gardening, walking, yoga and dancing at home to maintain some fitness. I know if I included more exercise, I could de-stress and release some pent-up emotions, but I do what I can.

There are many things we can do to overcome life's challenges more smoothly. I have got a few I can call upon now for burnout that may prove useful to others. Whatever comes up in our life, we ultimately want to move forward so we can live well again. I have found that always giving my energy away, did nothing to help myself, only others. I couldn't live well again if I was going to revert back to my old habits.

## Living Not Giving

I had to change and live in each moment, live to breathe and be more present.

Our life is made up of a series of moments and if we don't get through each well, then we will be stuck and won't be well enough to move forward.

Thich Nhat Hanh's philosophy on life says a lot about how we can try to live:

*"Live the actual moment.
Only this moment is life."*

## Chapter Eleven

# Chillout Inspiration

*"The universe is always speaking to us... Sending us little messages, causing coincidences and serendipities, reminding us to stop, to look around, to believe in something else, something more."*

(Nancy Thayer)

Amidst all the competing pressures the ordinary person contends with in today's busy world: from family, domestic duties and looking after children; your job, work pressures and deadlines; maintaining personal health and fitness; to managing appointments; preserving friends and social networks; and keeping up to date with emails, social media, news and information, we need to make more time, in among all those commitments, to give back to ourselves.

It's time to give ourselves some kindness and self-compassion through self-care. We need it!

Be inspired to chillout even more, during times of busyness and overwork, whether you're a mama, professional or student.

After experiencing burnout, I don't believe we can manage everything without maintaining our own balance. If you want to be engaged with the world and community and have thriving relationships and healthy family life, you have to be on top of all these things. But to manage them all well, we need to include some go-to chillout tools in our everyday life.

Because it's when we are the busiest that we need to tap into self-care the most.

If I can recommend anything, it would be to teach yourself to chill out before burnout happens. Discover what your needs are. Listen to your inner voice and develop a strong sense of what you need to do to maintain some deep inner calm, amidst your hectic life. Do what you need to do, to help yourself become more kind, compassionate and emotionally resilient towards yourself – whether it be adopting a meditation practice, doing some reading about mindfulness and the benefits of a mindful approach to daily life, or just etching out some quiet time to be still each day.

## Chillout Wisdom

There are so many resources available now to help busy people find calm and rebalance themselves. If you search online for information or free lessons on meditation, mindfulness, self-care and self-compassion, there is a seemingly endless amount. Based on the current climate of overworking, the fast pace of the 24/7 world and chaos of motherhood, let's face it, we all need some extra help to get through these modern world problems.

It took burnout for me to realise that I needed help.

So why not ditch your planning and organising, put your to-do list away for another day (it will always be there, believe me!) and just be still in nature? Many ancient cultures have a core connection to nature as a key place to centre themselves and chillout.

We can find some wisdom in how to connect with nature in the ancient teachings of Australias Aboriginal culture. They recognise the insight of deep listening through Dadirri. Dr. Miriam Rose Ungunmerr-Bauman, is an Aboriginal elder and educator from the Daily River region and wants to share the benefits of Dadirri. (Ungunmerr-Baumann, 2002)

Dadirri is about silent still awareness and the ability to focus on the outside, while listening to the inside.

We can let this information help us in our busy lifestyles. This way of listening to nature and being in nature, in stillness, is a belief system for Aboriginal people, akin to religion.

We all need more quiet-time being still in nature to find calm and gain some more balance. Just as nature needs time to restore itself to recover from droughts, bushfires and cyclones. We also need quiet time away from the expectations and commitments of our family and work to replenish our energy and nourish our soul.

It's a pity that our modern western culture places so little value on rest and on taking time out.

We're always busy and in such a hurry that our minds have little time to understand and listen to ourselves. This is important to learn what's right for us by connecting with our inner needs, whether it be the right job, the right relationship or the right place to live. Dadirri awareness understands that most of our pressures are ours alone – we place them on ourselves through our goals and ambitions.

*I think we could learn a lot from the ways of Dadirri in today's world. To live a more balanced life, to pay closer attention to our needs and be more grounded.*

Just listen, be still and see what you need.

New studies have uncovered that the natural world can improve our overall health and encourage self-reflection. (Williams, 2018)

It is believed that being around green plants, trees and leaves can have powerful benefits. Having access to green spaces outside a window, such as your home garden or local park can make us feel happier and healthier.

For our health and happiness, we need to value tranquillity more.

By finding a refuge away from busyness to immerse in our natural surroundings, we can replenish our energy and just 'be'. Simply sit in stillness while immersed in nature, whether it be near trickling water and or watching a dragonfly hover in your garden. We can all try this in our own backyard or nature park. Find an amazing spot to sit and consider your place in the world – it could be at an incredible tree or view overlooking the beach.

In Japan, people connect to the natural world by taking part in 'forest bathing.' (Qing Li, 2018)

They listen to the sounds of nature by noticing the movement of wind through the leaves and scent of the trees. Bathing in the sounds of nature allows people to reconnect with the world around them, reinstate a sense of calm and restore the lost art of effortless attention and soft fascination. (Qing Li, 2018)

The key to our wellness may be just outside our front doors, if we dare to look and pause, to really see what is there.

By thinking outside our own individual needs of work, family and expectations, to wonder at a natural phenomenon, whether it be a landscape or creature, makes us kinder and more aware of our own needs and that of the community around us. Julia Baird talks about the value of wonder and awe in her book, *Phosphorescence*. (2020)

She believes that when we marvel at something amazing, like a snow-capped mountain or striking sunset, it makes us think about things that are larger than ourselves.

It takes us away from busyness and into a quiet place where we can escape, to see the 'light within.' (Baird, 2020)

*By pausing to look and consider the mysterious and wondrous natural things that make up our world can put our busy lives into perspective.*

Our own self-care and compassion are often overlooked as it doesn't come naturally to give yourself kindness. But being kind to oneself and self-compassion are the keys to owning chillout wisdom. If we can be kind to ourselves then we would be more willing to give ourselves the time we need to nourish our inner needs.

Can you be kind to yourself, like you would be kind towards your best friend or a child?

If we treat ourselves with more self-compassion, we may value quiet time to be still more, to recharge from this busy world. If we practice self-compassion as a way of life, the benefits will flow - we could be more successful in other parts of our lives and feel more engaged in family life. It could assist your workplace achievements and you may find that you become more eager to form authentic relationships. (Neff, 2015)

If we are going to create a healthier society and find long-lasting personal wellbeing, health and happiness, we must place more value on the power of self-compassion. It may give you the balance that you need to help you to take a fresh perspective on the broader world, the way you look at life and how you move through your life, to live well.

**Chillout for Overwork**

The modern world is such a busy, demanding place. How did we find ourselves living in a world at this point in time, that is overflowing with work and travel opportunities, 24/7 access to technology and multiple commitments to satisfy? We tend to have a lot on our plates and often operate on autopilot to get through the onslaught of busyness. This is why we need to make time to relax and chillout. Without time to unwind and centre ourselves, we can very easily become overworked and exhausted.

*Our commitments and responsibilities are always there clawing at us. But it is up to the individual to choose to manage their own workload and what we say yes to.*

No-one else can do it for you.

We need to find the right break away from all these pressures to balance our needs for peace and quiet. We need to say no to doing extra things after work or in our precious lunch-hours to avoid health issues and burnout. Those times are there for us to recharge and reset our busy minds.

Depending on the type of role you have – the level of complexity and responsibility you manage – you may need differing amounts of wind-down and relaxation time. But everyone can readily access the three deep breaths, while they are looking out the window at work or sitting at their computer. You just need to stop what you're doing; I mean really stop and focus inward – it might help to close your eyes – then take a normal breath in and slowly breathe out. Repeat this three times and see how you feel. You can repeat this as often as you need to.

I believe that our personality type and whether you're a naturally introverted or extroverted person, will also influence how much wind down time we need. I'm more of an introvert and know that I need time alone to recharge myself and find my inner calm. I prefer to do things on my own, like go for a quiet solo walk outside in my lunch break, or a solo swim at the pool or beach.

*Something that has helped me unwind from phases of intense work or overwork, is to focus on the moment. When you are on a break from work, be intentional about really pausing any work-related mental activity.*

Take time to do a breathing exercise to transition your focus away from work. If you are preparing, unpacking or eating your lunch, try to focus solely on what you are doing.

For example, if you are chewing your food, focus on the flavour and texture of the food as a way to really get your mind off work. Changing habits can be hard and it might be tempting to check your phone, but it's really worth the effort to de-stress from your work and overthinking. When you try this for the first time, you may find it difficult – I know I did!

We don't always need to be with others, catching up at a café or having lunch in big groups. If you don't value your break, these work events will just eat into your wind down time. By the time afternoon arrives, you will probably have little energy left to focus on your work (without the help of sugar and caffeine). It might even help extroverts, every now and then, to have some alone time to chill out. It helps to stay grounded and connected to yourself while at work.

Mountain yoga pose can be done just about anywhere and helps to connect to the earth and focus on the present moment. You need to stand up tall with your feet hip width apart and focus on some mindful breathing. Breathe deeply and close your eyes. When you exhale, contract your pelvic floor and tummy muscles, then as you breathe in, relax and release. On the next breath lengthen the spine and repeat. Imagine your favourite mountain while you are doing it for increased connection and stability.

If you need to escape the office after a stressful meeting, why not give yourself five or 10 minutes to do mountain pose?

Balance is increasingly more important, as we manage our contributions at work. Especially as we work from home more, the lines between work and home-life have become blurred. All the hard work can take its toll with the many tasks, meetings, deadlines and professional relationships to manage. It is soul-crushing if after all that we gave in effort and hard work, we are overlooked – or our achievements aren't recognised.

We are just ordinary people juggling family and work responsibilities, yet we give a lot to our employer and workplace.

We can risk our health for our work contributions. An ordinary person puts their health at risk from working long hours (e.g. more than 55 hours a week), such as people who work full-time in a typical 9-5 job. There are known health impacts from this type of overwork, with these people having a 35% increased risk of stroke and a 17% increased risk of heart disease. (WHO, ILO, 2021)

No matter what level you work at, we know that the work we do can drain our energy to the point that we have nothing left to give. Managers and companies expect a lot of their employees today.

*We need to look after our own wellbeing and to give ourselves time to de-stress with kindness and self-compassion.*

Employers can push staff to their limits and often beyond their limits.

Sometimes we need to say no in order to protect our work-life balance and wellbeing. Sometimes it really is ok to not accept or take on work that we can't manage. That's ok. We need to make it ok for ourselves to do that. With so many tasks and responsibilities pulling at us, it's understandable that if we give too much to one thing, another part of our life will suffer.

So, let's give ourselves kindness to reach the right balance.

If we don't say no to the extra high profile and possibly career changing opportunity when it's offered, our family or health might suffer. Such incentives are enticing (I really do know this), but we need to choose them with care to ensure another aspect of our life doesn't suffer.

With the intensity and demands of our work combined with the expectations and duties at home, we really need to protect ourselves from exhaustion, and physical and emotional health impacts.

Today, we make ourselves available to the 24/7 world through our phones. Even if we don't work at night, many of us check our email or social media when we should be using the evening to rest and recuperate.

Finding the right balance between work and home is so important for our wellbeing. However, if we can find time to chillout even amidst all the busyness, hype and overwork, there are real benefits for our health.

So, let's do something about it.

Find the right combination of work, and balance it with time to give to YOU! Balance your needs with those of your managers. Your health is so important – we only have one life, one body and one soul to live. All we need to do is find the right chill out blend for our individual self and make it an important thing to include in our everyday life.

Chillout Inspiration

## Mama Chill

The invisible workload that modern mamas seem to manage, can be an overwhelming schedule of never-ending to-do-lists. Managing caring responsibilities, with our careers, looking after the family's health, making nutritious food – and the list goes on - means that we are always on the go. Always planning, thinking and doing. Today, it seems, mamas are more tired, stressed and less happy than dads. (Hogenboom, 2021)

Why can't we balance the needs of our family with our own needs? Why can't we say no to some of the extra, less essential things that deplete our energy and mean we end up giving too much?

We often juggle way too much in trying to keep up with our own work commitments, caring for our families and managing household tasks. Checking and replying to work emails, or preparing a presentation in between caring for our children, demands a lot of mental work. Some are able to manage it more successfully than others, but we don't all need to act like superwomen. Some of us really can't do it all – including me! We need to be self-aware of the impacts of this mental juggling act we do, otherwise we can step beyond our own limitations into overwhelm.

This invisible work can easily take a toll, if we aren't careful and more mindful!

It's hard to etch out any time for ourselves as mamas, when we are continually busy as we juggle work, with drop offs, appointments, school work and playdates (and more recently, working and schooling from home). So, let's try harder to etch out time to check in and centre ourselves. The boundaries between work and home have become more blurred with lock downs during the coronavirus pandemic.

It's a huge mental load that mamas contend with, which doesn't come without its impacts.

I come from generations of busy women and mamas. My grandmothers both managed huge families of four and five children respectively. These women organised the lives of their family day in day out, took care of their children, ensured they were happy, content and well-fed, as well as managing their household.

Growing up as their granddaughter – where their children had flown the nest many years before – it was rare to observe these older women taking a much-needed break except for a cup of tea or gardening (which was work anyway). They were – and still are – hard workers and I can't recall if they talked about how much they valued a break or if they talked about how overwhelming the burden of family life can be. They just did it and didn't complain.

It was very rare to see my own mum have a break away from family commitments just to be on her own to recharge.

We went to the beach in summer where we enjoyed time as a family, but I can't remember my mum saying she needed to relax on her own. She was always giving. The only time I recall she went away was to go to work or to do something for her siblings or parents. Even so, there wasn't the availability of yoga or meditation classes there is today, but these were my role models for how to best manage the motherload.

*Coming from this example, it was difficult for me to accept that I needed to give myself time to recover and fill my own cup if I am to adequately manage my own family's needs.*

Let's do better than previous generations and look after ourselves more. Let's give ourselves time to recharge and chillout when we need it. Find those things that are a good fit for us, whether it be exercise or stillness or a combination of both. Find a group of people who you can relax and chillout with, who you can be yourself with and let go of all imagined and real pressures.

One big change I have made to etch out time to do things for myself, is to schedule things in my calendar.

I can't manage my time well and do the things that are important for me, whether it be for work, interests or self-care, if I don't plan ahead. I never used to do this well, but now that's exactly what I do – I use my calendar more for scheduling tasks and me-time activities. Otherwise, the things that make me whole, calm and balanced, will fall by the wayside. Then I will become stressed, agitated and imbalanced all over again.

Letting go of perfectionism was an important step for me in releasing extra stress and pressure on myself.

Once I had released my hold on perfectionism and control in my daily life, the anxious feelings and tension I once had, dissolved. I held on strongly to my ideals around motherhood and how I thought I could raise my child. Things around bedtime, food, sleeping arrangements that all came from advice, but really created a perfectionist monster of a mama.

*When we accept that we can no longer control certain aspects of our lives around our kids, then you will find that some of your stress isn't there any longer.*

By the end of the day, about 4pm, I'm starting to run low on energy (as are many mamas).

But I have realised that if I don't find some time to rest and recuperate at this time of the day, before the dinner and bedtime routine, then I am less tolerant and shorter tempered. So now this is my time to just sit and find some stillness before I start dinner. So, I will set my son up for some quiet time, make a cup of tea and sit in the sun. Or I might do some calm breathing and quiet stretches or yoga to chillout.

## Chillout Inspiration

We can choose our own pleasurable moments.

I might get 15 minutes, or I might get five minutes, but it's carving out the time and focusing on you, that's an important step to create a new habit.

We satisfy the needs of so many as a mama that we often forget to look after our own. But let's also give ourselves what we need to live well and thrive. Let's not forget to satisfy our own needs as well, even if it's just for a few minutes at a time.

I love this quote from Glennon Doyle, which says a lot about what I try to aim for, as a mama:

*"What if a responsible mother is one who shows her children how to fight to stay wildly alive until the day she dies."*

## Chapter Twelve

# From Burnt Out to Chilled Out

*"It takes courage to say YES to rest and play in a culture where exhaustion is seen as a status symbol."*

(Brene Brown)

After experiencing first-hand the imbalance of work and life, the unreasonable expectations and pressures our employers place on us and the emotional load of motherhood, I needed to find a path forward through the numbness and lack of energy I experienced through overwhelm and burnout.

I came to see that burnout wasn't a failure or a fault of my personality, but a response to my upbringing and role models and the imbalanced structures and pressures of society – that probably began at some point during my education as an impressionable, young person.

The tertiary education system teaches us to succeed and compete, to continually push ourselves forward in a never-ending career journey without a real break to consider what we are doing to ourselves. It does not teach us that in continually pushing ourselves, we are potentially exposed to major health issues and overwhelm. Then, if you are continually giving too much, without dedicating enough time to recover, the result can be burnout.

Society does not teach us to balance all those things, to incorporate and value self-care as part of our daily rituals. Instead, we have to find our own way to that end.

**Final Thoughts**

My burnout was a product of living in a hectic 24/7 world in which I gave myself minimal breaks and time for myself, combined with my upbringing and my own unrealistic expectations and ambitions. At the time, I was also processing the distress and trauma I felt from the night it happened. I think because I was alone at night, with help out of reach, it left me a bit traumatised. It wasn't good for my sense of wellbeing because my safety was threatened. So, it took a while to get back to normal after that and feel safe again.

Looking back, if I could do anything differently, I would be more comfortable in my own company, spend more time alone and feel more content just being, instead of always doing. So I could have learnt how to rest and recharge well before burnout. I've always had a love of nature, which could have helped balance and calm me if I had tapped into it. But somewhere along the way, I forgot to notice and do this. I was always too busy and impatient and think I had a fear of missing out on my next adventure. I was always susceptible to the pull of exploring new and interesting things.

There are so many possibilities and distractions pulling at us in today's world.

These things can ultimately divert us from what we really need – inner stability, calm and peace. It's hard to pull back from those things to reassess what our inner needs are and find the balance between giving too much away and giving enough to ourselves. It's a bit of a trap because we can see so many exciting things that would fulfil us outwardly and be good for our careers. Unless we intentionally set aside time for self-assessment, we won't be able to redefine our true inner needs and find the right balance. I now know that in order to avoid overwhelm and burnout in today's busy world, we need to hold on to, and value true inner peace. So try to find, and hold onto, whatever it is that helps you maintain that.

If we believe those distractions – the overwork, the busyness and always-doing activity – are good for us, we won't be able to recognise their impact because we often feel satisfied and fulfilled. But maybe something is missing that you can't quite put your finger on.

*We aren't going to be able to recognise the impacts the exciting, enticing things might have on us, unless we intentionally make time for self-assessment.*

Sometimes, incentives pull at our ego and tell us it's good for our career or resume, but in reality, it could be detrimental or drain our energy. It's good to have a healthy awareness to these things, because they can be very enticing. They might be wrapped in colourful cellophane on the outside, but they might also have a nasty surprise waiting inside. That's what I discovered was waiting for me after I had spent all my energy unwrapping – burnout.

I gave so much of myself to university. I believed in my goals and studies wholeheartedly.

I believed in them so much that I forgot to remember myself and my inner needs.

It's here that I started to lose my balance. The bright lights of success and attraction of what might be possible, took me away from that. The bright lights blinded me and took me on a journey into another place where I could be anything, do anything. So that's what I did. I took a wild ride, had fun along the way, but the ride stopped abruptly in burnout.

I wasn't told that there would be a cost.

I wasn't told how to manage myself, maintain my balance and inner peace. My generation of women was encouraged to have it all. With all the sacrifices earlier generations of women had made for us, with all the striving and struggling they went through... We couldn't let them down, could we? So, we gave (and still give) everything we had in us, every ounce of energy, to satisfy those dreams of becoming career-women. Of becoming just like the men and competing with them on their stage.

Of achieving all of our dreams and being a mama, as well.

But there's a limit to that energy.

As professional women, we can't keep going like that. We aren't the superwomen we thought we could be. That kind of stamina is not for us. We can't maintain that kind of masculine energy day in day out.

Burnout taught me that. Something has to give. Our health or our inner stability or our relationships, end up crumbling away. All that you have studied for and planned for and the fun you had, can all collapse in a pile of crap, if we don't understand what it's doing to us. There is a price, unfortunately.

As women and mama's, we have to make our own individual choices about what's right for us.

I didn't understand my own limitations. I didn't understand that operating at such a high level can stress our system and eventually wear us out. The don't teach us that at university.

They don't teach us that to compete in a masculine world as a woman that we deplete our feminine energy. No, instead we end up stressing ourselves and not being kind to ourselves at all.

We expect a lot of ourselves.

No, we demand it as our right! In the end, the modern pressures and expectations we put on ourselves, are ours alone.

We have lost sight of what we really need and what we know deep inside. But it has been hidden. Forgotten. It has been trodden all over and pushed down by society, so it's completely smothered and hidden away. But it's still there, deep down inside of each of us.

It shows itself every now and then, if we choose to listen to our inner voice.

It's there in our uneasy feeling when we have been asked to do something we don't want to do or can't manage – the extra presentation or deadline that's been thrown our way. When we instinctively know that we can't do it, but we say yes anyway. It's there when our shoulders are so tight, they hurt when touched or when we roll them, because we haven't been paying attention to the fact we are stressed and need movement and relaxation to release it.

*I didn't know that if we pushed ourselves beyond our limits in our work without the balance of self-care that we could be exposed to overwhelm and burnout. But that's what that kind of incessant pressure, of achieving, competing and pushing ourselves to our limits, can do.*

After university, I forgot to enjoy the wonders of the world enough. I used to regularly escape through bushwalking and admire the amazing scenery that surrounds us. The act of bushwalking would allow me to focus on other less stressful things. I enjoyed that sense of being removed from the hustle and bustle of the world. If I had my chance again, I would try to include some of the things I used to enjoy as a way to relax and recalibrate, back into my daily life. I used to do field work as part of my job, but in the end, it's still work. Sometimes I was in nature, measuring, recording and calculating things. It's not quite the same as bushwalking for fun and relaxation.

Once, I loved to regularly go for bushwalks in Tasmania and immerse myself in nature. The diverse landscape, the weather formations, the changing seasons, the wildlife and forests. But once I started working after university, these things became a much smaller part of my life. I think that was a big mistake and if I could do it again, I would ensure that the things that made me feel grounded and present, were given a higher priority.

I let my career dominate my life too much, which created an imbalance. After moving to Canberra, the things I relied on to get me through the day weren't there anymore. I didn't try to replace them or find alternatives, I just let them go. That was a mistake.

I used to play music, too. I had a music in my bones it seems and learnt to play the piano when I was young, then the clarinet, then the saxophone in high school. Somewhere during university that all got derailed and I forgot to play music, which would have provided some balance and escape from my work.

Only after burnout did I take up the flute again.

We have a lot to teach our children and future generations about maintaining balance in today's busy world. How are they going to balance it all and recognise stress when it appears, when so many of us are struggling with overwork and finding space in our lives to chillout today?

As parents, we need to share what we've learnt about burnout and the pressures society places on us to succeed and achieve. We need to tell them that success can come at a cost if the work we do is not balanced or managed well. We need to tell them what works for us and what our own antidotes to stress are.

*Guide our children to balance work with energy-creating activities, rather than energy-depleting, or self-destructive ones.*

Raising children is not just about raising healthy, smart ones, it's also about raising resilient ones. Resilient children that can shoulder the stress of the modern world, rather than crumple under its weight. Let's share our wisdom and show them what we use to get through everyday stress with more balance. Make the habits we form part of their daily habits. Show them how they can choose one thought over another by meditating. Show them how they can release tension in their body through exercise, stretching and yoga.

Show them how they can find tranquillity and calm in nature and our green spaces.

Because being superwoman all day, every day, isn't showing our children the best way to live. It doesn't teach them the example they need to model, of a balanced mama and one who values chillout time as well as active time. I think it teaches them to give away their energy. It doesn't allow them to understand that they need balance in their life and that they also need to give to themselves.

I always thought there was something wrong with me when I burnt out.

So, I resisted it because I didn't want to think of myself as a failure. I just couldn't accept what was happening, with the mind-numbing fatigue, the twitching sensations, and the total change that had occurred within me. I didn't want to understand my issues, to deeply look at the truth, about the lack of self-compassion I had towards myself.

With a busy job always hammering away in my mind, I couldn't be still enough to listen to myself. So, I couldn't see what I truly needed. In a way, I was blinded or numbed to my need for self-compassion, to check in with myself and what my soul yearned for. But we really need to recognise the importance of being compassionate towards ourselves. Otherwise, burnout will floor you, as it did me.

I'm sharing my story so others can understand what I went through as a professional woman and mama today. I know that it will resonate with some and not others. I hope you can find some calm and inner peace in today's world and have the courage to work towards it if you are feeling overworked or overwhelmed.

Do it for your health and wellbeing – and for your family's, too.

Remember, it's time to stop giving and start living.

Reclaim the life you want and do things that replenish your energy rather than drain it. Let's create positive change; give more to ourselves and redefine our inner-most needs to prevent the ultimate game-changer: burnout.

# Afterword

### *Tranquil Hideaway*

Vividly and awakened, I see you in my dreams – so close,
You comfort me with your velvety warmth.
I see kindness and love in your calm, clear eyes
Although sometimes you're a distant memory
-my dreams bring you close to my heart.

In caves of crystalline colour, I feel stillness afresh;
Immersed in wide starry skies and cool alpine vistas.
Then I find a forest shelter of floating leaves.
And see alluring shimmering beaches ahead,
Where, fresh cleansing waves crash over me,
Effervescing, making me stronger; washing away my fears.

Then you are near again.

But from afar, I can remember it brightly when
We giggled and danced alone together in the moonlight.
You spun me around in joyous circles
Giddy with pleasure, I wore a magenta dress,
And your succulent scent infused my pores.

Forever, I know you will hold me in your arms
As you rock me and sing to me sweet soulful notes.
I now know I will never depart this wild place of my heart -
Know you would always be here, waiting for my return.
My tranquillity, my secret hideaway.

E. J. Mathews

# References

Baird, J., 2020, "Phosphorescence: on awe, wonder and things that sustain you when the world goes dark", HarperCollins Publishers (Australia), New South Wales, Australia.

Canavan, C., 2019. "Ever Graft Through the Night? This Is How Your Body Handles Shift Work", Womens Health Magazine. (https://www.womenshealthmag.com/uk/health/conditions/a26100721/shift-work-health/ ).

Hogenboom, M., 2021, "The hidden load: How 'thinking of everything' holds mums back", BBC News article (https://www.bbc.com/worklife/article/20210518-the-hidden-load-how-thinking-of-everything-holds-mums-back).

Neff, K., 2015. "Self-Compassion: The Proven Power of Being Kind to Yourself", William Morrow Paperbacks, 320pp.

Qing Li, 2018, "Shrinrin-yoku: The Art and Science of Forest Bathing", Penguin UK, 320pp.

State Government of Victoria, 2020, "Better Health Channel: Shiftwork", Department of Health, State Government of Victoria (https://www.betterhealth.vic.gov.au/health/HealthyLiving/shiftwork).

Johnson, M., 2021. "Nearly four in five Australians working from home suffered from burnout last year. Here's why", The New Daily (https://thenewdaily.com.au/finance/work/2021/01/15/working-from-home-burnout/).

Robinson, B., 2019. "Two-Thirds Of Workers Experienced Burnout This Year: How To Reverse The Trend In 2020" (https://www.forbes.com/sites/bryanrobinson/2019/12/08/two-thirds-of-workers-experienced-burnout-this-year-how-to-reverse-the-trend-in-2020/?sh=3354ebd27974

Smith, M., Segal, J., and Robinson L., 2020, Burnout Prevention and Treatment – HelpGuide (https://www.helpguide.org/articles/stress/burnout-prevention-and-recovery.htm).

Taylor-Kabbaz, A., 2019. "Mama Rising: Discovering the new you through motherhood", Hay House Australia, Sydney.

Ungunmerr-Baumann, M-R, 2002. "Dadirri: inner deep listening and quiet still awareness" (http://www.dadirri.org.au/wp-content/uploads/2015/03/Dadirri-Inner-Deep-Listening-M-R-Ungunmerr-Bauman-Refl1.pdf), © Miriam-Rose Ungunmerr-Baumann, All Rights Reserved, Emmaus Productions.

Williams, F., 2018. "The Nature Fix: Why Nature Makes Us Happier, Healthier and More Creative", W. W. Norton & Company, 304pp.

Whitbourne K., 2021. "Adrenal Fatigue: Is It Real?" (https://www.webmd.com/a-to-z-guides/adrenal-fatigue-is-it-real).

# References

WHO, 2019. "Burn-out an "occupational phenomenon": International Classification of Diseases", (https://www.who.int/news/item/28-05-2019-burn-out-an-occupational-phenomenon-international-classification-of-diseases).

WHO, ILO, 2021. "Long working hours increasing deaths from heart disease and stroke: WHO, ILO", World Health Organization and International Labour Organization Joint News Release, Geneva (https://www.who.int/news/item/17-05-2021-long-working-hours-increasing-deaths-from-heart-disease-and-stroke-who-ilo).

## *Appendix A*

# Resources

Antidote Yoga: www.facebook.com/antidote.dru.yoga

Anxious Mums (book): www.drjodirichardson.com

Beyond Blue: https://www.beyondblue.org.au/

Calm Meditation App: https://www.calm.com/

Dadirri Inner Deep Listening: https://www.miriamrosefoundation.org.au/dadirri/

Gidget Foundation (Telehealth Program): https://gidgetfoundation.org.au/get-support/start-talking-telehealth

Happy Mama Movement: www.amytaylorkabbaz.com/

Kendra Healing Arts (trauma sensitive yoga therapy): www.kendrahealingarts.com/

Parent Relaxation: www.trueparenting.net

Perinatal Wellbeing Centre (previously PANDSI): www.perinatalwellbeingcentre.org.au/

Reboot Your Health: https://inaturally.com.au/

Self-Compassion with Kristin Neff: www.self-compassion.org

Safe Work Australia: https://www.safeworkaustralia.gov.au/topic/mental-health

Transform Parenting: https://transformparenting.com.au/

# About the Author

Emma grew up in rural Tasmania, where she loved to ride her horse, go for bushwalks and camp at the beach each summer with her two siblings. Together, they built cubby houses, collected eggs and picked fresh apples and strawberries from the garden. Immersed in nature, Emma developed a strong connection to the Australian landscape and a passion for writing in her journal.

Emma's love of nature led her to study science at the University of Tasmania, where she obtained a Bachelor of Science with Honours. She started her professional career in Canberra and was dedicated to her work for many years, until it ended in burnout. Emma now enjoys a much slower pace of life and works from home as an author, freelance writer and mama.

Emma lives in Canberra with her husband and young son, where they enjoy exploring local nature parks together. When she gets time to herself, she loves to chill out and listen to music, write poetry, read Australian fiction and unwind at the beach.

In today's busy world, Emma is passionate about helping people manage the mix of work, kids, family and expectations. Knowing that burnout can happen in the blink of an eye, Emma wants to reach out to those who are overworked and overwhelmed, so they can access her practical solutions to de-stress, restore and refocus on a path to relaxation and self-care.

Even with so many demands pulling at us, Emma believes we can reclaim the life we want. We can do things that replenish our energy rather than drain it. Let's stand together to redefine our inner needs and give more to ourselves, to preserve our energy and prevent burnout!

Instagram @stopgivingstartliving
Twitter @EMDewDrops

# Acknowledgements

My book-writing journey really started at the Ultimate 48 Hour Author virtual writing retreat in May 2021. As a mama of a young person, still managing burnout, I had my doubts about how much progress I could really make towards completing my book. Then came a lockdown in the ACT and the two days a week I usually spent writing, became none. But I kept at it and bit by bit, I finally did it!

I am eternally grateful to the Ultimate 48 Hour Author team; Natasa, Stuart, Julie and Vivienne, for their guidance and tried-and-true book planning to completion methods, which supported me to keep going when doubt set in. Without their backing, I know it would have taken much longer for this book to see the light of day.

Also, it was such a pleasure to be part of the May 2021 Writing Retreat group. This is simple, this is easy, this is fun! Our shared journey and experience helped to motivate me through the ups and downs of book writing. We smashed it out!

A massive thank you to my band of readers who sacrificed their time to provide a testimonial; Ruth Wright, Gloria Lee, Amy Taylor-Kabbaz, Catherine McCoy, Kendra Boone, Thilini Wijesinhi, Kelly Wolf and Shannon Davey. I would also like to thank my Editor, Alex Floyd-Douglass, for her valuable feedback which has improved the completeness and readability of the book. Thank you to Nik Boskovski for working his magic on the cover, promotional graphics and related website.

I am so grateful to those who contributed their vulnerable stories of burnout, to help readers understand that burnout isn't as uncommon as we might think.

To my parents, for supporting me through this surprising journey and who gave the gift of peace and quiet at their place for my writing retreat. To my mum for her ongoing encouragement and for reviewing parts of the book.

I would like to acknowledge the Traditional Custodians of the ACT, the Ngunnawal people, and the NSW Eurobodalla Shire, the Yuin people, on whose land this book was imagined and transcribed.

Lastly, I am forever grateful to Roy for believing in me. For tolerating my demands for space and quiet when I wrote the manuscript and for truly helping me make this book a reality.

Achieving this book is real proof of overcoming genuine and imagined obstacles; to realise my dream of sharing my personal story with the world and becoming a published author.

# Offers for burnout recovery

**1. Stop Giving Start Living Playlist (freebie!)**

Find a quiet place away from whatever you're juggling today, to de-stress, unwind and chill out with some calming vibes on this playlist customised to calm a busy mind and escape feelings of overwhelm. Available for free on Spotify - https://spoti.fi/3OOFN9F OR QR code

*Got a song suggestion? Email stopgivingstartliving@gmail.com to make a request.

## 2. Grounding Visualisation ($19)

Listen to Emma as she helps you to quieten your active mind and reconnect to the earth with this grounding visualisation. Stand tall like a mountain and find your inner strength in mountain pose. In this accessible, 10-minute guided visualisation, you will start to be more grounded in the present moment and more mindful of your surroundings. All it takes is 10 minutes to restore some calm amidst the stress of daily life.

You can buy it here https://www.stopgivingstartliving.com/shop/ or QR code

## 3. Burnout Discovery Call - $39 - Introductory offer (usually $89)

Do you think you are on the road to burnout? Do you constantly feel exhausted and run-down? Have you lost motivation for things you usually enjoy? Are you always telling your loved ones how tired you are?

Ask Emma on this focused, one-on-one 30-minute **Burnout Discovery Call** - a mama and professional who has experienced burnout herself. Start to fast-track your recovery and live life fully again.

Readers of this book can make the most of this introductory offer, for your first session.

Make a booking via Calendly - https://calendly.com/emmamathews/discovery-call OR QR code

# Freelance Work

If you are interested in commissioning Emma for publication, you can find her on Instagram @emathewsauthor or her direct contact is emathews127@gmail.com.

# Self-Care Recovery Notes

## Stop Giving Start Living

# Final Word

I would love to hear from you if this book has made a difference and assisted your recovery.

If part of my story has had a significant impact on you, let me know - I value your comments!

Please send feedback to:
stopgivingstartliving@gmail.com

www.ingramcontent.com/pod-product-compliance
Lightning Source LLC
Chambersburg PA
CBHW021436080526
44588CB00009B/542